Praise for PassPorter®

I've been using these tips left and right. I feel I know a lot about Disney, and this book is AWESOME."

— Tina Kurtenbach in Oklahoma

I love all the information!

— Kim Caravello in Arkansas

Fun to read! Gets me in a Disney mood.

— Beth Spellman in Massachusetts

Good hints and tips on planning, dining, and touring the parks!

— Kaniala Gomes in Hawaii

I found so many new tips that I didn't have.

— Pam Copeland in Virginia

I really like a lot of the tips. There are some I could really use that I never thought of before!

— Tracie Carroll in Indiana

Love the tags that mark money saver, magic, kids, etc. Great overall tips!

— Marianne Goode in Illinois

Passporter's *Disney 500: Fast Tips for Walt Disney World Trips*
Edited by Jennifer Marx
© 2005–2010 by Passporter Travel Press, an imprint of MediaMarx, Inc.
P.O. Box 3880, Ann Arbor, Michigan 48106 • 877-929-3273
Visit us on the World Wide Web at http://www.passporter.com

ISBN-13: 978-1-58771-090-2
ISBN-10: 1-58771-090-0

Version 1.5 (printed in October 2010)

PassPorter's
Disney 500
Fast Tips for Walt Disney World Trips

Authored by PassPorter Readers
Edited by Jennifer Marx

PassPorter Travel Press

An imprint of MediaMarx, Inc.
P.O. Box 3880, Ann Arbor, MI 48106
877-WAYFARER
http://www.passporter.com

Table of Contents

Planning Tips 5
  Building Anticipation 5
  Saving Money 10
  Budgeting 12
  Finding Information 14
  Making the Most of a PassPorter ...17
  Scheduling 19
  Planning Together 24

Traveling Tips 29
  When To Go 27
  Driving 31
  Flying 33
  Ground Transportation 35
  What To Bring 36
  Packing 45

Lodging Tips 49
  Choosing Lodging 49
  Amenities 55
  Value Resorts 59
  Moderate Resorts 59
  Deluxe Resorts 60
  Disney Vacation Club Resorts 62
  Fort Wilderness 62
  Off-Property Resorts 63
  Miscellaneous 64

Touring Tips 69
  Passes 69
  Services 69
  Getting Around 70
  Itineraries 70
  Touring Tips 72
  Magic Kingdom 79
  Epcot 81
  Disney's Hollywood Studios 82
  Animal Kingdom 82
  Downtown Disney 82
  Water Parks 82
  Everywhere Else 83

Dining Tips 86
  Deciding on Dining 86
  Reservations 91
  Eateries 92
  Character Meals 97
  Dinner Shows 100

Making Magic Tips 102
  Magical Advice 102
  Tours and Classes 102
  Disney Characters 103
  Pressed Pennies 104
  Photographs and Memories 107
  Souvenirs and Shopping 110
  Trading Pins and Name Badges 112
  VIP Tips 113
  Special Occasions 116
  Holidays and Special Events 117

PassPorter 30% Discount 118
What is PassPorter? 120
Register Your PassPorter 123
PassPorter E-Books 124
PassPorter Online 126

© MediaMarx, Inc.

Planning Tips

» Order the Free Video

Order a free vacation planning kit from Disney at http://www.disneyworld.com. They ask your age for a reason. My husband and I got one that was designed for middle agers without small kids—and it pulls at your heart strings, reminding you of the Mickey Mouse Club, your mom and dad, your grandparents, and the wonder that is Disney. We get it out and watch it in anticipation of our upcoming trip and in remembering our last trip. To see Mr. Disney who never got to realize his entire dream—Disney World—a magical place where kids of all ages can play and dream!
By PassPorter reader Susan B.

» Play Sing·A·Long Videos for Kids

To give your younger child(ren) an idea of what Walt Disney World is like, I have found the live-action Disney Sing-A-Long videos to be very helpful. Beach Party gives you a glimpse of Disney's Hollywood Studios, the various water parks, and the Polynesian Resort. The Camp Out video shows bits and pieces of Fort Wilderness and Pioneer Hall. The Disneyland Fun video, although obviously filmed at Disneyland, still gives the child a sense of what some of the rides, sights, and sounds will be like. Flik's Musical Adventure at Disney's Animal Kingdom highlights the lands of Disney's Animal Kingdom.
By PassPorter reader Melissa M.

» Countdown on Your Computer

We keep a countdown clock on our computers that show the amount of time before the trip to keep everyone excited. You can get a free countdown clock at http://www. magicalmountain.net. The PassPorter Boards also have a built-in countdown clock for your upcoming trip.
By PassPorter reader Charlotte H.

» Letters from Characters

Our last trip to Disney was also the first for our two children. So my wife decided to make the experience for them really special. About 1 ½ months before we were scheduled to leave, my wife had the kids favorite Disney characters "write" them a letter (on character themed letterhead she created) and she mailed each of them a letter once a week. Each week the kids would get a letter from Cinderella, Snow White, Sebastian, Simba, Goofy, and of course she saved Mickey & Minnie for last. The look of joy and excitement on the kids faces was worth all the work she put into this. It also drove the kids nuts! Wanting to leave for Disney each day they received their letter. It was the perfect build up for the kids and to be honest, their excitement got my wife and I just as excited to leave.
By PassPorter reader Blair

Planning Tips (continued)

» Dress Up Dollars in Mickey Ears

To get the kids excited about the upcoming trip, try dressing their allowance money with Mickey ears. Cut out the sticky part of a post-it note in the shape of mouse ears, color it all black, and put it where appropriate on Mr. Washington on a dollar bill! This is much more versatile than Disney dollars.
By PassPorter reader Daniel B.

» Break Out the Photo Albums

Get out your photos from previous Disney trips (or ask family and friends for theirs). This really helps you get in the mood. It also helps you remember your most favorite spots at Disney that you want to be sure not to miss on your next trip.
By PassPorter reader Caryn S.

» Read Trip Reports

I read trip reports found on the web with my family. I print out as many trip reports that meet our criteria. Then I gather the kids and my husband in the den and read the reports aloud. We find not only good information, but some humor as well. Everyone in the family gets to be a part of the planning process. Trip reports can be found at http://www.passporterboards.com, http://www.disboards.com, and http://www.allears.net, among other places.
By PassPorter reader Susan M.

» Give Disney Dollars as Goodies

We are planning our Disney trip for next May. In order to keep the excitement up for my kids (it seems no one is ever as excited as me!) I give them Disney Dollars to be used for buying their goodies when we finally get there! I use them for Valentines Day, for Easter in plastic eggs in their baskets, rewards for good report cards, etc. Use your imagination! The kids are always excited to get them and we have found from many past experiences that they are much more careful spending their "own" money than they are with Mom and Dad's!
By PassPorter reader Melissa S.

» Make the Countdown Fun

This is our first trip to Disney and we are getting more and more excited each day. Our excitement has spilled over to our three-year-old daughter. She has asked us each day, every hour on the hour, "Are we going yet?" Not having any concept of time, I borrowed an idea I got at Christmas a couple of years ago. I made a paper chain with the number of links equal to the number of days left until we go. Each night at bedtime she rips off one link, when all are gone, we leave to see Mickey! Not only is she excited about the trip, she also goes to bed much more willingly. Two Birds, One Stone.
By PassPorter reader Lesa S.

Planning Tips (continued)

» Get Everyone Excited With a Disney Kit

About a year ago, my husband and I planned a Walt Disney World vacation for our family (there were eight of us in all) and our favorite planning tip comes from the time we spent getting this trip organized. We had recently returned from Disney but the family members coming with us on the trip we were planning had not been since the early '80s. To get them familiar with the new Disney and to get them excited about spending eight days there, we put together Disney Trip Kits to give as gifts about six months prior to the trip. The Kits included maps from all of the parks so our guests could familiarize themselves with them prior to arrival (we had brought these back with us from our last trip), a guide to Disney that included notes on restaurants so they could help us plan where to eat and when, a small notebook for recording places they wanted to visit and eat, and a character washcloth.
By PassPorter reader Dodie W.

» Get Name Badges in Advance

You can purchase Disney Name Badges and an album that holds pressed pennies at http://www.laughingplacestore.com. I've always wanted my son to have a name badge like the Cast Members wear, but we've never seen the place to purchase one at the parks. He loves the pressed penny machines, but the pennies usually get misplaced because of their size. I ordered these two items before we left so I didn't have to spend time looking at the parks.
By PassPorter reader Vicki

» Hunt for Vacation Fun

To get the children familiar with the Disney parks, have them choose a theme (i.e. Mad Tea Party), then have them go on a scavenger hunt with a map of Walt Disney World to find food to eat throughout the day. This way, the child learns how to read a map, explores different foods, and becomes familiar with the parks layout. This is probably best for kids 7–10 or older. If you're short on time, narrow it down to breakfast, lunch, or dinner and just one area of the park. When I did this with my boy's at Disney, we had ice cream for the main course (the theme was Main Street) and it was lunch!
By PassPorter reader Elizabeth L.

» Get in Shape For Your Trip

To ward off tired feet or lessen the strain while still prepping mentally for the excursions to come, I've found myself exercising to Disney tunes. My favorite is Disney's Millennium Album. There is nothing quite like walking for 20–30 minutes to the beat of "Reflections of Earth." Time flies while I'm getting in shape and I'm ready to go.
By PassPorter reader Bonnie W.

Planning Tips (continued)

» Learn Before You Go

What makes our Walt Disney World trips so magical is learning about what Disney has to offer before we get there. Then each night we talk over what worked that day and what did not work. We look over the map for the park we are going to the next day and get familiar with what is there. I tell the kids about the food and the rides. This helps them feel comfortable. Then that day we do what ever we want!
By PassPorter reader Susan R.

» Send Weekly Updates to Traveling Companions

We are taking our extended family with us on our next trip to Walt Disney World. Since they've never been before, I've been sending them weekly updates via e-mail to psych them up! I've sent them links to Disney sites (like PassPorter.com), advance dining reservations, countdowns, as well as fun facts about Disney. It's kept us well connected and psyched for our next trip in June!
By PassPorter reader Chris D.

» Chart Chores for Disney

Our Disney trip is planned for May. For the three months previous, we have a chart on the refrigerator for our 6-year old-daughter. To get excited about our trip and to minimize school/work day early morning hassles, each morning before we leave, we check off each morning responsibility that she has. i.e., get dressed, brush teeth, pick out day's snacks, make sure backpack is ready, etc. At the end of the week, if she has five days worth of checkmarks, she earns money for Disney. This goes into her basket along with her birthday/tooth fairy money to be spent only by her in Disney!
By PassPorter reader Tami R.

» When to Tell the Kids

A big decision for us when planning a Walt Disney World vacation is "how to tell the kids we've decided to take them to Disney World." We toy with the idea of someday not ever telling them until the morning of the trip. We envision gently tapping on the shoulders of our two daughter's at the awful hour of 4:00 or 5:00 am and have them groggily stir to hear us saying "WAKE UP, WE'RE GOING TO DISNEY WORLD!" Of course we will have packed for them in secret. Since we always long for a Disney vacation in February or March when it's still cool (or downright wintry) where we live in Massachusetts, we could easily get their spring/summer clothes packed without the knowing. Of course the other way is the route I've succumbed to so far. That is telling the kids when we're certain the vacation will definitely take place. Then we spend the next months and weeks watching our free vacation planning video, old movies of prior vacations at Disney, and planning, planning, and planning. The anticipation of the trip is almost as good as the trip itself...
By PassPorter reader Shelley

© MediaMarx, Inc.

 = money-saver   = time-saver   = magic-maker   = kid-friendly

Planning Tips (continued)

» Get DisneyTime

Download Disneytime at http://www.disneyzone.net/countdown.htm. It is a great way for you and your family to countdown to your trip!
By PassPorter reader James F.

» Make a Countdown Board

Before every trip to Disney World we make a countdown board. We purchase a piece of white posterboard and decorate it with disney stickers, pictures, or the names of our favorite attractions. We start 200 days before our next trip and each night before bed we each make one line to "x" out a box! On our countdown calendar we also keep track of important dates like when our final payment is due, when to make dining reservations, and to confirm any other reservations. We also mark special days with disney stuff to do. Like, watch the travel video again, look at our scrapbooks from past visits, or home movies from Walt Disney World. Not only does it help us keep track of the important dates, but it reminds us every day of how much closer we are to Disney World!
By PassPorter reader Jessica S.

» Lose Weight for Disney

I'm escorting several disabled adults to Disney World this winter. Two of them have been told to lose some weight before they go. We have weigh-ins twice a month and they get a Disney Dollar for every pound they lose. They have to pay if they gain. So far, the two of them have lost 15 pounds in two months!
By PassPorter reader Pam P.

» Listen to Disney Radio

If your husband thinks you've been to Disney enough and should see other places, this tip is for you! Introduce your husband to the Disney radio station at http://www. srsounds.com. I did this and my husband now listens to the Disney music online. It wasn't more than a couple of months and we were scheduling a trip to Disney! The magic of Disney music reminded him of the wonderful times we have had at Disney and we was the one ready for yet another trip! Of course, I'm always ready!
By PassPorter reader Debbie A.

» Kids Create a Vacation Book

Make a Vacation Book with your children before you leave for your trip. Help them decorate the cover with the vacation dates and drawings or Disney stickers. The booklet works best as a fold and staple type. The left side can have space for the following each day: The highlight of my Disney day; The low of my day; What we did; What we ate; and Who we met. This information can be filled out while unwinding each night of vacation. The right side would be for autographs. Leave plenty of pages for a few photos and postcards to be attached. The booklet will fit in moms' purse easily. This makes the anticipation for the trip just a bit easier!
By PassPorter reader Nanci P.

= money-saver   = time-saver   = magic-maker   = kid-friendly

Planning Tips (continued)

» Surprising a Child

© MediaMarx, Inc.

When I started planning our November Disney World trip I knew I wanted to make it a surprise for our seven-year-old daughter. After all, it's the trip we've been promising her AND it's for her birthday—having it be a surprise would make it even better! I immediately hit upon a couple of problems, though. I was too excited about the planning to not talk about Disney and I wanted to know what some of her preferences/possible fears were. So, I hatched my plan! I told her that we (she and I) were going to surprise Daddy with a birthday trip to Disney! Now we talk about rides and restaurants all the time and she doesn't suspect a thing! She even knows we have reservations at Pop Century (which she really wanted to try), she just thinks they're for a few months later than they are! Even Daddy's in on the plan—he pretends to like all the same things that she does so it only seems natural that we'd be planning to incorporate them. It's wonderful to be able to plan this trip with her without ruining the surprise!
By PassPorter reader Alicia D.

» Staying in the Mood

We play Disney music at least once a week to keep the magic and visit the Disney Store to just stay in the mood. Besides, we visit the store often enough that we hit some really good sales.
By PassPorter reader Charlotte H.

» Try For Discounts

If you have a Visa card, are a Florida resident, or in the military, inquire about discounts when you call Disney Reservations.
By PassPorter reader Kathy J.

» Purchase Passes In Advance

Purchase your park tickets before leaving for your trip. This eliminates standing in line and wasting precious time. You can purchase park tickets in advance at http://www.disneyworld.com or at trusted third-party ticket brokers such as http://www.undercovertourist.com, http://www.ticketmania.com, http://www.floridaorlandotickets.net, and http://www.mapleleaftickets.com.
By PassPorter reader Kathy J.

= money-saver   = time-saver   = magic-maker   = kid-friendly

Planning Tips (continued)

» Shop Before Your Trip and Save

As I prepare to go to Walt Disney World this October with my husband, his brother, my mother in law, and our 4 ½-year-old niece I've started buying items that she will ask for when we get there. I found boxes of those glow stick bracelets at the store for about a third of the price that you will pay for at the fireworks or late night parades. Also since we will be there just before Halloween I'm checking at second hand shops for "princess" or Disney costumes which during anytime of the year little girls will want to wear at the "World."
By PassPorter reader Cindy G.

» Comparison Shop

The first part of planning is to get a rough idea of where you want to go (e.g. moderate resorts in my case). At this point I contacted multiple travel agents, Disney, and AAA to get quotes on what I wanted to do. All this information can be confusing. Everyone has a slightly different package they want to sell you, so to sort it all out I put all of that information into Excel to make the comparisons easier. Then I knew exactly who to call to get the best deal on my vacation and was sure I knew what all of my options were.
By PassPorter reader Brendan

» Use Disney Rewards

This credit card from Chase gives cardholders special discounts on Disney resorts, packages, and tours, plus onboard credits on the Disney cruise. The card itself has no annual fee and earns "Disney Dream Reward Dollars" equal to 1% or more of your purchases. You can redeem your dollars relatively quickly for Disney travel, entertainment, and merchandise. Exclusive cardholder benefits are also typically offered, such as special character meet and greets. Another perk is the "pay no interest for 6 months" offer on Disney packages and cruises, but keep in mind initial deposits and all payments must be made with the card or you can lose the deal. Be sure to read the fine print carefully, too—if you carry a separate balance while floating a 0% vacation deal, your payments may apply to the higher interest balance first and you could end up paying some steep interest. Also, double-check exactly when you need to pay off the balance and be careful about confusing terminology. We have a Disney Visa ourselves and we think the "rewards" are just average, interest rates are high, and the available discounts are sparse (but attractive when offered). Disney Rewards Visa is available to U.S. residents only. If you have a Disney Rewards Visa, be sure to mention this when making reservations so they can offer any available incentives or deals. For details, visit http://disney.com/visa or call 877-252-6576. Also see our in-depth article at http://www.passporter.com/credit.asp.

Planning Tips (continued)

» Fund-Raise For Your Students Trip

I teach and I am taking a group of students to Walt Disney World over spring break. To raise money, the girls bring baked goodies to my room each morning and I sell the treats to my students for $.50 each. Since September, the five students have raised nearly $500 each, which has more than covered the cost of their airfare and their hotel room. If you teach, you might see if you can host such a fund-raiser in your own room. Or, if you know a teacher, see if he or she can host the fund-raiser for you (offer to share the profit, of course).
By PassPorter reader Sherry S.

» Save Money During the Year

We clip coupons all year and buy snacks and drinks (that won't go bad) so that we don't have one large grocery bill before we leave.
By PassPorter reader Charlotte H.

» Budget for Souvenirs

To avoid overspending, create a souvenir budget for everyone in the family. Before the vacation, the kids earn their souvenir budget by doing chores and such. It makes their prizes from Disney World seem a lot more important since they know they earned it and spent their own money on it. Of course a little help from the parents is permitted when the time actually comes. But remember your budget!
By PassPorter reader Tiffany B.

» Disney Dollars Help You Save

I have trouble saving money for my trips. I'm a terrible shopper and love to spend, especially at the Disney Store. So whenever I need to save for a trip to Disney, I go to the Disney Store every paycheck and buy Disney Dollars. That way I can buy something at the store and satisfy my urge to spend while still saving money for the trip. Those Disney Dollars are cute and fun to spend. I also give them as gifts to friends and family who are going on trips to Disney.
By PassPorter reader Mandie

» Keep the Change

We learned my husband had to go on a business trip to Florida and decided we would combine a short (4-night/5-day) Walt Disney World vacation. We told our children to save any and all "silver" change they received or found and placed it in the handy change jars we keep around the house. Three days before our vacation they could roll it and exchange it for cash. They could split it three ways and spend the money on whatever they wanted to purchase at Disney. Let me tell you they saved very well, each child had $85 to spend any way they wanted. It added to their excitement for the trip, saved us going crazy saying "no," and taught them the value of saving change. They can't wait to see how much they'll save for the next trip. Don't start too soon or they may lose momentum and the excitement!
By PassPorter reader Kathy F.

 = money-saver   = time-saver   = magic-maker   = kid-friendly

Planning Tips (continued)

» Pay Some Allowance in Disney Dollars

During the months before our Walt Disney World trip, I gave my oldest child a little bit extra each week with her allowance, this extra was in Disney Dollars. This ensured that she'd save this money for our trip and also gave her a little something each week to add to the excitement. Then while in Disney if she wanted something beyond what I'd pay for she had extra money of her own. It gave her a little control and eliminated much of the "buy me, buy me" talk. If she wanted something I didn't feel was a good buy, I'd tell her she could pay for it if she really wanted it. Also made her think twice about buying something because she really wanted to have it to spend her own money.
By PassPorter reader Dianne G.

» Use A Piggy Bank to Save Money

In order to save our spending money, my husband and I get an inexpensive piggy bank. The bank cannot be opened unless it is broken. We periodically fill it with coins and bills. When it gets to be a week before our trip we break it open, count the money and immediately cash it into traveler's cheques or Disney Dollars. Last time we had over $1000.00! That was all we needed. (OK, we saved for a year, but still!) This really helped cut costs because we didn't realize how much we saved up! So our entire vacation was paid for before we even set foot on the plane!
By PassPorter reader Anne K.

» Set A Souvenir-Buying Policy

To avoid bad cases of the "gimmes" with our kids while at Walt Disney World, we set a souvenir-buying policy before we ever leave home. We tell them each what their souvenir allotment is for the trip, and also tell them that none of us will buy any souvenirs on the first day we are in the "World." We spend the first day looking and admiring all of the new goodies we see while touring, and they go back to the hotel that night debating over which one they would most like to have. By giving them time to think their choice over, they end up making a selection they're happier with in the long run. This technique has helped us avoid buying an item on the spur of the moment and then seeing something later that looks better! It also helps teach the kids to operate within a budget and to use good decision making-skills.
By PassPorter reader Shari A.

» Set Goals as a Family

This will be a trip for the entire family, so it is up to the entire family to plan and save for it. Each child and adult in the household (we total six) is pitching in the money saving and attraction planning. We are trying to show the kids that you can set a goal, save, work hard, and in the end, enjoy!
By PassPorter reader Annamarie S.

= money-saver   = time-saver   = magic-maker   = kid-friendly

Planning Tips (continued)

» Bank Your "Found" Money

To save money to pay for meals on our Walt Disney World trips we have a large ceramic Mickey Mouse bank. Everyone in our house refuses to spend change and at the end of the day we all put this "found" money in Mickey. Every month we take our proceeds to our bank and they run it through their coin machine. Then we are off to The Disney Store to purchase Disney Dollars which come in nice strong envelopes. When we get home we decide which meal we will pay for with this month's savings and write the name of the restaurant and the date and advance dining reservation number on the envelope. These are all kept in our safe and by the time our annual trip comes around we have many meals already paid for!
By PassPorter reader Elin H.

» Read for Disney Rewards

I wanted to give my son a total of $200 over the next nine months (for our Disney trip) but wanted it to be a reward. In an effort to encourage my son to read, I used upcoming special days, such as birthdays, Christmas, and Easter Sunday to inspire him. If he reads 50 books by his birthday he will receive $50. If he reads 35 books between his birthday and Christmas he will receive $50 and lastly if he reads 30 books between Christmas and Easter he will receive $50. From Easter Sunday until we leave on our Disney trip if he reads 25 books he will receive another $50. He is learning and he does not even know it. If your child is like mine and hates to read but loves money or loves rewards and you want to find a way to supply them with Disney money for their upcoming trip then this is the way to go. At least it is for me.
By PassPorter reader Ursula H.

» Prepare Tips Before You Leave Home

Are you always fumbling around looking for those bills to leave a tip for that wonderfully helpful cast member, housekeeper, or town car driver? Well, don't! We make up Disney tip envelopes before we leave home with Disney themed clip art on them and fill them with the appropriate tip. On the envelopes for the housekeepers, we note the day on them. Envelopes for the town car driver get a "thank you" for taking us to Disney and for returning us safely home. Just throw the ready-made tip envelopes in your purse or backpack and you always have the correct tip right at your fingertips!
By PassPorter reader Bobbi Jo G.

» Keeping Quarters for Video Games

Here's a good tip for those traveling with video game nuts! On our last trip, I told my 9-year-old son that on our downtime back at the hotel he could go to the arcade. He filled an M&M tube with quarters (they fit perfectly!). The deal was when the money ran out, so did his time at the arcade, and we wouldn't add to his supply. He made those quarters last the entire week we were there!
By PassPorter reader Ellen G.

= money-saver   = time-saver   = magic-maker   = kid-friendly

Planning Tips (continued)

» Organize Your Budgeted Money

Before our trips, I get a coupon organizer and label each section with the day we are going to be on our trip and a family members name. Then I put the amount of money we've budgeted (usually traveler checks) in each section.
By PassPorter reader Debra G.

» Give Kids Disney Presents

For all of my children's birthdays and holidays, they received gifts for our Disney vacation. Aunts and uncles bought Hoop-De-Doo Revue tickets and a dinner at Rainforest Cafe. Grandparents bought the park tickets. And we gave Disney Dollars. With six children this helps with the money part and the children (even the three-year-old) knows how much money they have and look forward to the trip with more anticipation.
By PassPorter reader Karen R.

» Research Discount Codes Online

Check out all the discount codes the following sites have been most helpful to include getting me here to PassPorter. Good discount sites include: http://www.themouseforless.com, http://www.mousesavers.com, http://www.allears.net, http://www.intercot.com, and http://www.wdwinfo.com. BIGGEST Tip: Buy your PassPorter guidebook first—it will give you info immediately that may take forever to find anywhere else.
By PassPorter reader Brian H.

» Plan Your Trip Early

Buy a travel guide like PassPorter and start planning your trip early, at least a year in advance. Make your reservations for a Walt Disney World Resort at least six months in advance. Also visit message boards like the ones offered by PassPorter and ask lots of questions. Don't wait until the last minute.
By PassPorter reader Teri W.

» Your Library is a Gold Mine

I went to our local library and reserved most of the Walt Disney World travel guides they had available to use to plan what attractions we want to visit with my young daughter. They also had a file on Walt Disney World that contained many brochures and maps from the park which were helpful to see while planning. By using the library and only buying the PassPorter for reference, I saved myself quite a lot of money. I made notes in my PassPorter from the books I had borrowed and also made copies of the maps to put in the pockets. Very helpful and cheap!
By PassPorter reader Shawn K.

© MediaMarx, Inc.

 = money-saver   = time-saver   = magic-maker   = kid-friendly

Planning Tips (continued)

» Ask for Names

When making any type of reservation—hotel, restaurant, etc.—also get the name of the person you are speaking with. This will help in the event of a problem.
By PassPorter reader Laurie R.

» Research is the Key

In the past eight years, I have become a true fanatic when it comes to Walt Disney World. I have read every book that was and is on the market (PassPorter being number one on my book list), and I pretty much thought I had enough information to make me a Disney travel agent. In fact, my family members and friends always came to me to help them with their Disney itinerary. It was when I started web surfing that I realized where the real wealth of information is found. Web sites such as PassPorter.com, DIS discussion boards (http://www.disboards.com), and MouseSavers.com have saved me an enormous amount of money on each trip that I book. By doing a little research, it becomes very easy to stay at the best of the hotels (even getting concierge service). My tip is to do lots and lots of research on your own. It can save you loads of money and gives you a hands-on feeling regarding your vacation.
By PassPorter reader Pam E.

» Create Your Own "Tips" Database

When planning my first trip to Walt Disney World in over 10 years, I loved reading all the tips and tricks on the PassPorter site and every other site I could find. Every time I found one that made me think "I need to remember that!" I copied it to a Word document on my computer desktop. When I was packing and doing my final planning, all my favorite tips were in one handy document that I printed out and shared with the rest of the adults in my group. We all loved it! Here's how I did it: Create a Word document called "Disney tips," save it to your computer desktop, when you see a tip you like use the mouse to "cut and paste" a copy of the tip, open your document and "paste" it in. Viola! You have a personalized Disney tip sheet that you can put right in your PassPorter.
By PassPorter reader Stephanie S.

» Knowledge is Power

While planning our trip I scoured the message boards, which are a great resource. No sales spiel and real people with real experiences! I open a page in Notepad and copy and paste things that I think are interesting for future reference. I keep a page open on my desktop labeled CHARACTERS, PARKING, DINING, TICKETS, etc. This way I can find the tidbits of knowledge as I need them. It's the worst to know you saw something on a discussion board and not be able to remember the details or find it again. Knowledge is power but not if you can't remember it.
By PassPorter reader Dawn A.

Planning Tips (continued)

» Up To The Minute News on the Web   [SAVE!]

We use the Internet a great deal to help in planning our Walt Disney World trip. By checking different Disney-related web sites, it brings us up to the minute news about special rates, park hours, etc. It also provides a forum to meet others who share their love of Disney!
By PassPorter reader Jan T.

» Research Resorts Online

Don't be afraid to ask questions on the discussion boards regarding resort questions. You can read the replies on the boards, so you don't have to give your e-mail address. There are many Disney regulars who love to share their information with you—the more specific the question, the more direct the response. Ask about atmosphere, kid-friendly resorts, locations of properties (on and off Disney) and where to stay within the properties. Also, check Disney web sites often as you plan your trip (such as http://www.passporter.com, http://www.allears.net, http://www.mousesavers.com—you can get discount codes for rooms and other Disney needs here). You never know when the right discount or tip may show up that fits your needs!
By PassPorter reader Cynthia J.

» Ask the Locals!

Ask cast members, water park guides, and other Orlando residents for advice! They often know the best places to dine, newest spots kids will love, and other gems.
By PassPorter reader Jackie P.

» Keep Lists of Disney Links

Look for lists of Disney Web site links. I have found frequently when researching on the Web that each web site has it's favorite links all listed on one page (even PassPorter.com). Print out this list and use it for future research and more ideas. I have stumbled across some of my best information on sites found via another site.
By PassPorter reader Kim L.

» Get a Guidebook for Kids

Even if you're an adults-only group, pick up *Birnbaum's Walt Disney World for Kids* guidebook. It's jammed full of great tips, things to do while waiting in line, and where to find Hidden Mickeys. There's a space in the back for autographs and places to record special memories! I pick one up every year!
By PassPorter reader Barbara O.

[SAVE!] = money-saver   [Speedy] = time-saver   [Magic] = magic-maker   [Kids] = kid-friendly

Planning Tips (continued)

» Invest in Trip Planning

Take the time to do research. Too many people try to do Disney on a "whim" and end up missing a lot and spending even more. Every year I take at least two vacations to Disney and I still take the time to find the best price. My PassPorter has been the best investment because all my notes and tickets are located in one place. NO MORE SEARCHING!
By PassPorter reader Lisa

Note: The next eleven tips involve the PassPorter guidebook. If you don't have one, just skip to the next relevant tip.

» Highlight Of Your Trip

I sit down with my PassPorter and a yellow highlighter, along with lots of plastic paper clips. If I see something that is important to me, I'll highlight it for quick access later on, and clip the page. I have a zillion clips in my book for our next trip!
By PassPorter reader Lin F.

» Stuff It

Prepare envelopes for the different aspects of your trip (travel, lodging, park visits, etc.) to organize those portions. When you check into your room, put the travel portions in the wall safe since you won't need them for a few days at least. You can also use PassPorter's organizer pockets. It unclutters much of the aspects of your trip so you can enjoy it while you're there.
By PassPorter reader David S.

» PassPorter in the Potty

I recently toured the parks with a PassPorter Deluxe edition. It was fantastic! The only time it was inconvenient was when I had to go to the restroom. Where should I put my book? I recommend that folks take about 20 inches of thin soft rope or yarn and thread it through the binder. Tie a good firm knot on the outside of the PassPorter and you have a carrying handle! This is perfect for hanging on a hook inside the bathroom stall. [Editor's Note: Hey, if you need a bathroom-handle for your PassPorter, why not? Maybe we should add a new "bathroom compatibility feature" to future PassPorters?]
By PassPorter reader Stephen G.

» Add Note Pages to the PassPorter

I bought the deluxe edition of PassPorter and I love It. After adding in Note Pages (printed off your web site, thanks) I found my PassPorter getting bulky. Your book helped me choose my resort, so now I removed the resort pages and bound them with two snap rings until after my trip.
By PassPorter reader Shannon

SAVE! = money-saver   Speedy = time-saver   Magic = magic-maker   Kids = kid-friendly

Planning Tips (continued)

» PassPorter Page Markers

Use the Post-it Tape Flags to mark the pages of your PassPorter that you use the most, such as the resort you chose, the page on the rides of the park you will be visiting that day, the eateries, etc. With the flags you can write notes on them such as "index" to quickly find it. Another alternative would be to use colored paper clips.
By PassPorter reader Catherine P.

» The PassPorter Works!

Use the PassPorter! It is truly amazing. We have had Birnbaum's guide every year and it is okay, but the reading is dry. I find PassPorter much more fun. I plan to take the relevant pages out each day to stick in my backpack so I have a handy reference in the parks. I haven't put it down for the last couple of weeks. One of us is always quoting from it.
By PassPorter reader Claudia S.

» Laminate Your PassPorter Maps

After purchasing the refill pages for our Deluxe PassPorter, we hated to throw away our old pages. We then got an inspiration. My husband and I spent a little "therapy" time coloring the wonderful fold-out maps with our daughter's colored pencils. We then trimmed them down and laminated them with self-adhesive laminate sheets we bought from Wal-Mart. We plan to punch a hole in the maps and tie them onto our stroller when we visit the parks in January. No more digging for a map, unfolding it, and then refolding it!
By PassPorter reader Jo

» Let Kids Decide Where To Go

Buy a PassPorter book and let the kids go through the different sections of the park and decide what all they want to see and do. Have them put their initials aside of each attraction and when they're done you can plan what everyone wants to see.
By PassPorter reader Cheryl Z.

» Color Coding Your PassPorter

When we first used our PassPorter for the trip, my daughter, my husband and I each took a different color from a box of colored pencils and went through the PassPorter to mark what we wanted to do. It was easy to compare what items were the most popular and then organize what to do and not to do.
By PassPorter reader Corina D.

= money-saver   = time-saver   = magic-maker   = kid-friendly

Planning Tips (continued)

» Highlight of Your Trip

I highlighted the map legends and the corresponding places on the fold-out maps for the four major theme parks. Green for the parade routes, blue for the rivers canals and lakes, Pink for the bathrooms etc. It made it quick and easy to locate what we were looking for.
By PassPorter reader Sharie S.

» Separating Kids from Adults

Last year when I bought the PassPorter we decided to travel with our best friends that have a seven-year-old son. I took sticky tabs that were of different colors and "marked" the parts of the PassPorter that pertained to the adults and to the child. When the boy wanted to do something for himself, he just took my PassPorter and flipped to the pages that were color coded for him. From there he picked an attraction that he could do. This allowed everyone the feeling that they had an input in our trip. We never had a complaint out of him the whole five days.
By PassPorter reader Jennifer M.

» Plan Practically

Plan ahead. Research so that your vacation is all you want it to be. Be practical—don't plan more than you have time for. Plan a couple of BIG activities and the rest is all bonus. This way you and your family are not disappointed that you didn't see/do everything on your "to do" list. And most importantly, relax. You are on vacation!
By PassPorter reader Tausha

» Plan! Plan! Plan!

People think I am crazy planning our Walt Disney World trips over a year prior, but that is the only way you are guaranteed to get the perfect Walt Disney World vacation. Rooms need to be booked a year in advance, restaurants require three or months prior. Newbies to Walt Disney World don't realize that you cannot just show up and get a seat for special programs or restaurants. I read the PassPorter thoroughly and used it to keep track of when I need to call for advance reservations during the year before our trip. Otherwise we wouldn't be able to enjoy the best food, best lodging, and best times of our lives!
By PassPorter reader Cat K.

» Take a Break Everyday

Always allow for a break each day. If you over exert yourself then it does not make for a good vacation. By the time you return home your feet will be aching and your entire body will feel worn down. Relax and take it easy!
By PassPorter reader Romy

= money-saver   = time-saver   = magic-maker   = kid-friendly

Planning Tips (continued)

» Schedule Alone Time

When traveling with adults, give yourselves alone time. Think about it: when we're at home, most of us don't spend 24/7 with the person/people we've touring Disney with. We usually work in different places or have different activities that we do on our own. Even the best of friends/lovers/significant others can start to get on each others' nerves when they spend all of their time together. That's why I recommend taking at least one morning or afternoon when each person does their own thing. It can be really refreshing to do this and trust me it really helps to keep your Disney vacation magical. You'll have new things to share and to talk about when you meet up again plus I find that I tend to meet more new people when I'm on my own and there are always some really interesting cast members and guests at Disney.
By PassPorter reader Pam K.

» Get Homework Out of the Way

Since I have been known to pull my kids out of school to travel to Walt Disney World (shame on me!) I insist they do their homework before we go. I ask teachers to send home the work they will miss. The night before while I am packing, the kids are in their rooms doing homework and out of my hair. I don't have to lug their books along. This also allows them to enjoy their vacation, knowing their work is done.
By PassPorter reader Jennifer

» Scheduling is King

Make sure you plan enough time for each park. Having to rush around and "skip" attractions makes for a hectic vacation and you leave with regrets. If you cannot plan enough time—schedule, schedule, schedule. Have a game plan on what to see and stick to it—make the most of your vacations. Most importantly remember that Walt DIsney World is NOT all about the theme parks. Take some time for a nice dinner, a luau, a boat ride, etc.
By PassPorter reader Maryanne

» Little Calendar for Big Ideas

A little calendar for the month that we will be in Walt Disney World is invaluable. I like to paste it in the inside cover of my PassPorter, but it'd also work taped up anywhere you'll be able to see it often. I've referred to my little Disney planning calendar so many times! It helps me keep my advance dining reservations straight, figure out Extra Magic Hours, decide which day to go to which park, etc. If you make a calendar for your trip, be sure it has enough space to make little notes on.
By PassPorter reader Kristen C.

» Whiteboards Work

Use a huge whiteboard! Putting it right next to my books, computer, and copious notes on Walt Disney World really helps me plan and switch around days and activities until I get just the right combination.
By PassPorter reader Neal L.

 = money-saver   = time-saver   = magic-maker   = kid-friendly

Planning Tips (continued)

» Plan Ahead and Eat Early

Plan your days out so you can go to each park per day and if time allows you can go to other attractions around the area. Eat your dinner early about 3:00 or 4:00 and you will get lunch prices, and a small treat at 6:00 or 7:00 will be all you will want. You will have more money to spend on other activities. Planning ahead will make your trip more enjoyable.
By PassPorter reader Sue R.

» Making the Most of a Short Vacation

If you are taking a three day vacation in Orlando with kids, and can only visit Disney World one day, wait until the third day to visit a Disney park. This allows small kids to get a good night's sleep the night before. Many kids need a night or two to acclimate to a hotel and will be tired the first and second days. There are many other things to do the first couple days like water parks, etc.
By PassPorter reader Laura B.

» Relax Your First Day

Don't go to the parks on your arrival day! By the time you check in and get sorted out it's after noon. You'll waste a full day of your pass on half a day worth of fun and you'll be tired (and irritable) by dinner time. We spend that first afternoon and evening on "outside the park" stuff like checking out the pool at the hotel, going to the grocery store for the weeks snacks, eating dinner, and shopping in Kissimmee. The miniature golf courses at Walt Disney World are a fun idea, too!
By PassPorter reader Dawn A.

» Plan Special Activities

We are Walt Disney World veterans but we never grow tired of our vacations. Each time we plan a visit we buy ALL the books, again, since there's bound to be a change. Then we each read through our guides and make a list of everything that we would like to do. From that list each "child" (they're all young adults now) is allowed to pick one special event, be it parasailing, diving, a backstage tour, whatever they would like. By doing this we break up our long days with some other activity which we all enjoy and most importantly which we all share and for which we have great memories. A soft smile comes to my face as I remember the many times my "stepson," who is now 17, has told me that the day he did DiveQuest is still the best day of his life ... thank you Uncle Walt.
By PassPorter reader Susan G.

» Don't Get Up Early Too Often

Choose only a few days to get up early!! Keyword there is "few"! (Also, a swim in the pool, if there is one, is very relaxing. But don't forget your goggles.)
By PassPorter reader Josh D.

Planning Tips (continued)

» Make Memories For Your Kids

If you know that you can't make Disney a regular vacation in your family (because of cost), plan on at least two trips once when your kids are small (between the ages of 4 and 8) and again when they are older (between the ages of 11 and 15). The young children still believe in everything and it is quite wonderful to experience it with them. While the young teens aren't as innocent, Disney has enough magic to enchant any age, making this a great vacation to share with your young teenagers. Creating new memories that will last a lifetime and recalling some of those wonderful memories from when they were little.
By PassPorter reader Karen G.

» Flexibility Is The Key

The best thing I can recommend to anyone planning a Walt Disney World trip is flexibility. It is so tempting to fill in all the blanks on our PassPockets with reservation numbers, to-dos, and must-sees. But there are so many factors at work, from the stamina of the weakest link in your group, to the weather, to, Heaven forbid!, illness, that it is easy to be thrown off your "perfect" itinerary at a moment's notice. My advice: Roll with the punches! Don't be afraid to reorganize or cancel and remake reservations! Go ahead, spend a whole day relaxing at your hotel until the upset stomach goes away! Go ahead, take that nap while the little ones nap, too! After all, this IS a vacation. Most of all, don't get upset that your itinerary is ruined. Think of it as customizing your vacation! After all, there IS always next time.
By PassPorter reader Priscilla P.

» Plan A Little Each Day

When planning to visit the "World," it can be an overwhelming job, but, also a trip in and of itself. Many people get two vacations in one: one in the planning and then when the real thing comes. Create a timeline to get things done. Set dates and do something towards your trip everyday. Even if it just to review your PassPorter or check out a new web site. That way to continue to build your excitement. You also don't get to Disney (or worse yet, back from Disney) and hear about something and wish you would have done that. This way you've researched things thoroughly and you'll be able to plan your dream vacation!
By PassPorter reader Missy D.

» Laminate Your Schedule and Tips

I scaled down and laminated all of our daily disney schedules and PassPorter tips for each park. I used a more dense 4x6 photo size laminate which made it water proof and easy to carry. I highlighted our favorites by color coding, bold print, and used "FP" for FASTPASS attractions and the best time to see each attraction. I broke it down by sections of the parks. I included restaurants, special notes, things to look for such as Hidden Mickeys, least-crowded restrooms, etc. I always had our PassPorter nearby for a detailed reference, but these laminated cards were kept out as we toured.
By PassPorter reader Terry M.

= money-saver   = time-saver   = magic-maker   = kid-friendly

Planning Tips (continued)

» Index Your Trip

We make an index card for each day before we go. These are very easy to carry in a fanny pack. Our tentative plans are on there for each day including reservations with the confirmation numbers and restaurant phone numbers. Everything is written in pencil in case changes are necessary which usually are. You have to make yourself flexible due to many factors including weather, travel delays etc. We also leave all our travel/hotel information back home in case of emergency. Save all your index cards for when you get back home. Make notes on what worked and what didn't and what restaurants you liked etc. Keep a folder marked Disney and then when it is time for the next trip you can refer back to them. You always think you will remember something but in all the excitement of planning the next trip past things are forgotten. You need to be organized to make the best use of your time.

By PassPorter reader Robert M.

» Be Out of Touch

My favorite tip for touring Walt Disney World is DO NOT leave your "REACH" number with your boss or with your assistant! It's okay to be out of touch on your vacation.

By PassPorter reader Mickey S.

» Save Magic Kingdom for Last

If you are traveling with younger children be sure to take them to the Magic Kingdom last. That way they won't be disappointed that the other parks may not live up to the excitement of the Magic Kingdom.

By PassPorter reader Jenny A.

» Excel at Attractions

I keep a list of every "attraction" in every park (I include shows as well) in an Excel file on my computer. Each family member lets me know their top five favorites, not to miss things for each park. We then compare the notes and use these forms to start planning our itinerary.

By PassPorter reader Charlotte H.

» Use Networking Sites

On my most recent trip, my traveling companion and I lived 1000 miles apart. I used a networking site to create our own special web site specifically for planning all the details of our trip. I used the calendar feature to remind us about when to make advance dining reservations and kept track of all reservation numbers and many other details of our trip. We also posted little status reports to each other during the planning process. And there is even a place to post pictures once you return. [Editor's Note: These days, the best networking site for this type of planning is Facebook at http://www.facebook.com.]

By PassPorter reader Lori T.

Planning Tips (continued)

» Empower Everyone

Make each member of your party a copy of your schedule for the trip. It could include the park you plan to visit, reservation numbers, pre-arranged meeting times, show times, etc. That way, if somebody gets lost, they will know where to meet up with the rest of the gang without disrupting touring plans.
By PassPorter reader Rebecca V.

» Bring Your Folks

Ask Grandma and Grandpa if they would like to come with you. There are plenty of things for seniors to do and when it is time to put the kids in bed they are usually ready to go too. This gives Mom and Dad a chance to head back out to experience Disney at night. We did this and it worked especially well!
By PassPorter reader Beth W.

» Get Kids Involved

With kids, planning a trip to Walt Disney World can be almost as enjoyable as the trip itself. I have a son and a daughter and my wife and I placed a generous portion of the daily itinerary planning on them. But first we ordered and downloaded as much Disney information as we felt would give them a good feel for the park attractions. Take advantage of the free promotional video offered and call the 800 number to order it. Then using park maps, your favorite Disney vacation guidebook, and the video. Let your kids plan out an itinerary for the number of days in the parks. Start them with a block sheet with some times entered and then have them work alone. Bring them together and compare and contrast. I think you will find, as I have, that their likes and dislikes are not all that different. The kids develop a sense of "ownership" of the trip planning and are anxious for their plans to become reality. We found it enhanced our trip tremendously, while filling the time of a lot of anxious days leading up to our trip.

© MediaMarx, Inc.

By PassPorter reader Tad K.

» Get Organized!

Organize, organize, organize!! Have everything in one place (like your PassPorter) and make sure all the details are attended to before you get there. Then you can relax and enjoy your trip. (My family doesn't call me the Disney Commando for nothing!)
By PassPorter reader Sue K.

= money-saver   = time-saver   = magic-maker   = kid-friendly

Planning Tips (continued)

» Get Your Group's Input Before You Go

This tip works well for particularly large groups. Buy a couple of guidebooks (including PassPorter, of course!) to Walt Disney World, including one with lots of pictures for kids. Have everyone go through and put a small sticker or marker dot (each uses a different color) on the attractions, activities, and places they most want to do/see. Then compile everyone's answers and create a chart or spreadsheet that will allow you to easily see what the group's overall and individual priorities are and organize your daily outings accordingly. Everyone gets equal input and everyone goes home happy. (Be sure to allow for changing priorities once you get there though! Guidebooks never really prepare you for the real thing!)
By PassPorter reader Sherri

» Compare Notes with PassPorter

My sister-in-law and I each buy a PassPorter and we go through them on our own and mark what we want to do. Then whenever we get together before our trip we compare notes to see what we agree on. We do this for restaurants and rides both. This helps us not to miss the must see's and do's and also makes our trip start that much sooner because we start planning the minute we receive our new PassPorter. We have already started with our new copy!
By PassPorter reader Nancy F.

» Planning Trips for Large Families

We have made several trips with "extended" family. We are the chief planners and as such we take an informal survey of likes and dislikes. We prepare the others with updates, make all the arrangements and save a lot of time on the actual trip. Taking all the information into account, we make a brochure of our personalized trip, by computer, including graphics. It is a great hit with everyone because we build in special requests! We lists "don't miss" attractions a suggested itinerary and give special attention to the one or two "command performance" activities. We are also experienced in what the kids are going to want to do. Armed with this information, families are free to come and go as they please. The cousins are on a similar track and the parents are warned a head of time about what and when. The itinerary is flexible and since we range in age from 7 to 85 years we are free to explore or sleep in at will with out feeling left out or trapped into someone else's idea of a good time. We are also able to plan our individual days around the one or two "group" activities or reservations that are set. My advice, keep it simple and plan for everyone's comfort. We have found the kids like to hang together and one set of parents go with them part of each day, with the communal camera. This leaves others time to spend alone for a romantic lunch or dinner and the kids can't wait to join up again and tell their folks about what they did. I think nothing is more enjoyable than hearing "Mom, you just gotta do this tomorrow." This gives everyone breathing room with a few important events for group photos and remembrances. Bon Voyage!
By PassPorter reader Noel P.

© MediaMarx, Inc.

SAVE! ↑ = money-saver   **Speedy** ↑ = time-saver   **Magic** ↑ = magic-maker   **Kids** ↑ = kid-friendly

» Hold Family Meetings

We had two family meetings before the trip to go over the calendar of events and to make sure everyone is aware of what has been planned while we are there. Plus it just made us excited about the trip.
By PassPorter reader Loni S.

» Take Everyone!

Take all the family members (or friends) that you know would enjoy it and want to be there. Don't leave anyone behind, if you can avoid it. My mother and I went together but left my father and brother home in Canada, because of work & school responsibilities... and we felt guilty during the whole vacation for having as much fun as we did. We tried to have LESS fun, in fact, often repeating, "OH, I wish those guys were here." It took several years before we were able to go again, but when we did, we even took as many aunts, uncles, and cousins as could join us. The Disney experience is better when shared!
By PassPorter reader Jody M.

» Create Photo Cards

I went online and found different pictures of different parts of parks. I made them into cards about the size of baseball cards. I then laminated them. On the back of each card I printed clues and facts without giving away location. I then hooked about 5-10 "cards" on a stretchy key ring and gave it to my girls. So as we were walking around they could "find" the destinations on the cards. The kid with the most finds got to pick what was for dinner that night. They learned the park and learned neat facts about different parts of the park. It was very inexpensive entertainment and they look around more at their surroundings instead of rushing to get somewhere all the time. We took enough to do 3-4 days worth and they are now great keepsakes.
By PassPorter reader Bobbie T.

» Give Plans to Everyone

I photocopy the worksheets from PassPorter. Then after filling them out with the final plans I copy them again and give then to everyone in our party. They then can look over the sheets while in the car or plane traveling to Disney. I even copied, cut and the restaurant reviews and then pasted them in order we were going to them for my sisters. They loved it! I put the reservations on the sheet and carried it with us.
By PassPorter reader Susan R.

© MediaMarx, Inc.

SAVE! = money-saver   = time-saver   = magic-maker   = kid-friendly

Planning Tips (continued)

» Calendars for Group Trips

I was the main "planner" for our family trip which spanned four generations in age. We utilized the dining option package. After getting as much information about each restaurant in advance as possible, we arranged a Sunday meeting where all gathered and made decisions on the table meals. Each person chose one special meal/restaurant that they wanted so all were happy. We also checked out counter meals and made some decisions. Finally I made a "calendar" of our week of dining with information on the where and when as well as the reservation numbers where needed and time to arrive etc. in each box. I ran a copy for each person in the group and then color coded each box on all copies before distributing them. It took hardly any time at all to do. At a glance one could see that table meals were in yellow, counter meals were in pink, and meals not on plan were in green, snack options were in blue. It was easy to carry with us and has become a scrapbook souvenir besides. Also each box had a small bit of room to write a note or two for memories, comments, etc.

By PassPorter reader Linda M.

© MediaMarx, Inc.

Traveling Tips (continued)

Traveling Tips

» Tie Dye T-Shirts

We have three children ages under the age of 7 at the time of our trip. I'm an advance planner, so waiting and anticipation was very hard for all of us. Because we were also taking my Mom and the three kids, I assigned specific colors for everyone to wear each day so I could keep up with them. My special magic was a project that the kids and I did when we had exactly one week to go before our trip. We tie-dyed everyone a shirt, the kids had t-shirts and the adults got polo style shirts dyed. The thing that made them special was the Mickey Mouse design that we did by rubber banding the shirts with one large central circle and two smaller circles for the ears. They turned out great and you could really see the Mickey Mouse impression on the fronts and backs of the shirts. We also painted everyone's name on the bottom of the shirt. We wore them on Animal Kingdom day and it really helped to set us apart. They were the perfect thing to wear for the Kali River Rapids rides because we got soaked, but since we were in tie-dyes they still looked respectable! The kids got a big kick out of proudly telling the cast members and other guests that we made them ourselves. The kids still say they are the best souvenirs we have from the trip and wear them all the time. *By PassPorter reader Pamela S.*

» Two Trips on One Pass

Make your Disney ticket money go farther by buying an annual pass and planning your visits to give you two trips on one pass. For example, plan your first visit for August and your next for June or July. *By PassPorter reader Deborah G.*

» Be Prepared for Florida Weather

Florida weather is extremely mercurial—one minute it can be hot and sticky and the next still hot and sticky but pouring down rain. It rains almost every afternoon especially during the winter. Be smart and bring your own raingear or buy early once the rain comes as the lines can get terrible. Or, plan to have somewhere to duck into for a few minutes. The rainstorms generally don't last too long, so don't let a little water ruin your whole day! *By PassPorter reader Elika P.*

» Go the Week After Thanksgiving

Travel to Walt Disney World the week after Thanksgiving, if you can. We went at that time one year and had virtually no wait for Tower of Terror. We experienced very short waits for many other rides, including Maelstrom, China, The American Adventure, Pirates of the Caribbean, etc. The Christmas decorations are also out in full force at this time. *By PassPorter reader Mark J.*

SAVE! = money-saver   **Speedy** = time-saver   **Magic** = magic-maker   **Kids** = kid-friendly

Traveling Tips (continued)

» Go in the Weeks Before Christmas

The best time of year for a Disney vacation is the weeks before Christmas (but not Christmas itself). The park is beautifully decorated for the holidays and pictures turn out great! We always use a great photo for our greeting cards when we get home. Also, the weather is fantastic for those of us that mind the heat of summer in Florida. Kids love to get away from school for a long weekend in November and the park is much less crowded.
By PassPorter reader Amy P.

» Pack for Chilly Days

When going in the winter months, ignore the five-day forecasts that say it will be 85 degrees and sunny! Always pack a winter outfit (or long underwear) and a hat and gloves. We were there last Dec. 15-23. It was 85 the first day and felt like sub-zero the rest of our trip. We bought sweatshirts, gloves, and hats inside the parks! However, it was still magical and glorious!
By PassPorter reader Elizabeth W.

© MediaMarx, Inc.

» February is Fab

We traveled in February to see Walt Disney World. The lines were shorter and the weather was not bad. Two other friends of ours traveled during this time before spring break hits and had a similar experience. Try it!!
By PassPorter reader Lori F.

» Travel the Third Week of August

For travelers visiting Disney in the summer months, I found the third week in August is less crowded. Florida kids have already gone back to school by this time. Also, the deluxe and Disney Vacation Club resort room rates typically drop to value season rates by this time. *[Editor's Note: Just check that there isn't free Disney Dining during this time period, or it will be crowded!]*
By PassPorter reader Micky P.

» Diamond is My Best Friend

On two occasions when I purchased my park passes at my AAA office, I received a AAA Diamond Preferred Parking Certificate. It provides the opportunity to use the special parking areas at the Magic Kingdom, Disney's Hollywood Studios, Epcot, and Disney's Animal Kingdom theme parks. These lots are close to park entrances. The certificate much be presented with a valid Walt Disney World Resort identification or valid theme park ticket.
By PassPorter reader Kathy J.

= money-saver   = time-saver   = magic-maker   = kid-friendly

Traveling Tips (continued)

» Fun Car Trip Ideas

Before our trip (in the car for 8 hours), I prepared a box wrapped in Mickey paper, filled with Minnie and Mickey Beanies, coloring books, earrings, necklaces, and games—all with the Disney theme. This box not only occupies the kids but everyone got something—yes the adults, too. Sleep shirts, boxers, socks—if you look around you can find some great Disney merchandise close to home to start out your trip. When we arrived each person was given Disney pajamas as a reward for not saying "Are we there yet?" A complete road map was prepared with a highlighter, indicating the starting point and ending point. Each child mapped out what they thought would be the best route, and then watched to see which one we would take. Each child was given a $10 roll of quarters and each time they were rude to another member of the family it cost them—they had to put a quarter into a jar. If they kept a good attitude and did not cause trouble as kids sometimes do in the car, they got to keep their money. Otherwise, the money in the quarter jar became property of Mom.
By PassPorter reader Bennea S.

» Bring Glass Markers on Car Trips

If you're driving to Disney, bring dry erase or special glass markers for the windows of your car. Drawing on the windows is a fun, no-mess way for kids to pass the time.
By PassPorter reader Linda B.

» Cheap Source for Goodies

An inexpensive source for items to give kids who are anxious or impatient during travel is Oriental Trading at http://www.orientaltrading.com. The item doesn't have to be much; small car, ring, or crayons. It's getting to unwrap a new thing that seems to do the trick!
By PassPorter reader Terri

» Remember Where You Parked

When parking at Disney parking lots, you are told to park in a particular spot with a name such as "Goofy 97" or "grumpy 23." This name can be VERY hard to remember, so purposefully pick the most forgetful member of your party and challenge them to try and remember the car parking number every day throughout your stay, possibly providing them with a small prize at the end if they complete it successfully. Trust me, this gives you something to have a good laugh at every day when you sadly walk away from the park. Who couldn't laugh when watching their friend/family member vainly struggle to come up with the car space name in order to win their 'prize' at the end of the week! Plus no-one notices when you yourself totally forget it! But seriously, write the name down as soon as you park! You can even write in your PassPorter, or why not take a digital picture of the parking lot sign?
By PassPorter reader Jenny C.

© MediaMarx, Inc.

 = money-saver   = time-saver   = magic-maker   = kid-friendly

Traveling Tips (continued)

» Countdown the Car Trip

We make a countdown paper chain for our traveling time. I determine how long our trip will take from the time we leave the house to the time we arrive at our hotel in Orlando, then divide this into 30 minute increments. Then I cut paper strips, about 1 $^1/_2$ inches wide and 4-6 in long. My children and I will count our one strip for each 30 min. increment, then we make a paper chain. As soon as we leave the house we start the "time" and the kids get to tear off a chain every 30 minutes. It's great because the kids can see how much longer until we're there!
By PassPorter reader Cindy W.

» Spread Out Your Trip

Spread a long car trip out over a couple of days. We usually take three days down and three days back by staying with friends and family that we wouldn't otherwise see. We plan other site seeing stops along the way as a means to stretch our legs and enjoy spending time together even if we're stuck in a car together for eight hours a day for three days straight. The most important thing to remember when traveling together is to have fun and enjoy being together no matter what you do or how you travel!
By PassPorter reader Chrissi R.

» Use Internet Travel Sites

Check out http://www.travelocity.com, http://www.expedia.com, etc. for cheap fares on car rentals, airfare, hotels, and more. I saved up to $500 booking separately. That's a lot of extra spending cash.
By PassPorter reader Donna B.

» A Mobile Scavenger Hunt

When we drive to Disney with children, I make up a scavenger list with items the kids must see along the way including license plates, types of vehicles, restaurants, etc. and any signs or historic sites. The first one who finishes his list on the way gets a Disney T-shirt and then there are other prizes for the runners up. The kids love it.
By PassPorter reader Linda L.

» Entertainment on the Road

On our car trips to Disney, we take along a 9" AC/DC TV with DVD player and headphones so my granddaughter can watch Disney films along the way. What's great is that the sound can only be heard by her. Now Granny can listen to the radio as she watches her favorite movies. Also, I have organized all of her play activities in front of her seat with a lap desk, coloring books, follow the dot books, car bingo games, and all of her play dolls at arms reach.
By PassPorter reader Donna F.

= money-saver   = time-saver   = magic-maker   = kid-friendly

Traveling Tips (continued)

» I-95 Information Source

Since we drive from Jersey, I always check out this site for I-95 information continuously until the day we leave: http://www.usastar.com/i95/homepage.htm. *By PassPorter reader Traci*

» Curb the Car Blues with Disney Jeopardy

We always drive to Disney and it takes us at least 20 hours to do so. When the kids get bored and start poking at each other, I get out my homemade version of Disney Jeopardy! I usually have four or five categories (Disney music, Characters Movies, and The Theme Parks) and I invented my own questions from 200 points to 1000 points in each category, just like jeopardy. The kids love playing this—it gets them excited and takes their minds off of the boredom of being in the car for an hour or so. The winner gets Disney Dollars! (Of course the other child earns the same amount of dollars in some other manner being a good sport, helping with luggage, or what not so each child has the same amount of money). I found this to be great fun for me as well thinking up all the questions prior to our trip! *By PassPorter reader Kristi K.*

» Check for Airfares on Wednesday Night

If you need a flight to Disney, call your preferred airlines at 12:01 am on Wednesday mornings (one minute past midnight on Tuesday). This is when many airlines release their new fares! In addition, this is when courtesy holds that weren't converted into tickets are put back in the system, which can mean better availability for you. [Editor's Note: Early Wednesday morning is also when airlines e-mail their specials, too. Don't overlook checking airline web sites on Wednesday morning either.] *By PassPorter reader Kimberly K.*

» Happy Kids = Happy Flight

To ensure our son never becomes bored on the plane ride standing in attraction lines and at meal times, I always have small "surprises" in my backpack. A few months prior to our trips I look for small, inexpensive items that will occupy him in a pinch. Some of the items used previously include spinning tops small puzzles and maze games, finger puppets, yo yos, matchbox cars, small action figures, plastic army men, etc. I go out to the party store and buy some inexpensive cellophane party bags and place the small toys in them. I put a few in my backpack everyday while at Disney and if my son is getting restless in a line or during dinner, I can pull out the small treats. It really does the trick. During our last trip we were dining at the Rose and Crown Pub and awaiting the start of IllumiNations while dining on the patio. Since we were stretching our dining time out I pulled out some new micromachine cars for our son to play with. Not only did these occupy him for the next hour but they also occupied a five-year-old sitting at the table next to us. His parents were very grateful! *By PassPorter reader Charissa Z.*

= money-saver   = time-saver   = magic-maker   = kid-friendly

Traveling Tips (continued)

» Watch Your Time Zone

If you're flying in from the West Coast and you have small children, keep your watches set to your time zone and not Florida's. This way you aren't forcing any children to wake up to get into the parks. Also you are eating at off times for most locations so there is less of a wait.
By PassPorter reader Laurie

» Curbside Check-in Save Times

At the airport, use curbside check-in for your luggage. Usually there is no line and you don't have to lug your luggage into the terminal. You can then go straight to the gate and check-in there to get your boarding pass. [Editor's Note: Be aware that some airlines have a mandatory fee for curbside check-in, and it's considered polite to tip for good service at curbside.]
By PassPorter reader Karen H.

» Make Travel Fun Again

When traveling to, from, or around Walt Disney World, treat the transportation as if it is an attraction of its own. Get excited about the plane ... when landing or taking off—put your hands in the air like you would on Rock 'N' Roller Coaster. When traveling by car, look at all the sights around you like it was Kilimanjaro Safaris at Disney's Animal Kingdom. The traveling is much more fun this way!
By PassPorter reader Renee S.

» Relax Before Returning Home

We always like to get a late afternoon or early evening flight home so we can maximize our vacation time. After a long day in the parks and/or by the resort pool, we prefer to shower before our flight home. To accomplish this, we booked a "Body Polish" at one of Disney's spas a couple of hours before we left for our flight (any spa treatment would work). This gave us full use of the spa facilities, steam room, shower, hair dryers etc. We left for our flight as relaxed and peaceful as can be!
By PassPorter reader Connie M.

» Stay Busy on Flights

When on the plane make sure to stay as occupied as possible. (Unless you plan to sleep, of course.) As the saying goes, "time flies when you're having fun." So even grownups should bring a few things to do. Keep in mind that the longer you're on the plane, the more playthings you should bring.
By PassPorter reader Anthony D.

Traveling Tips (continued)

» Fly With Rule 240

I love this one! When you are at your airline's departure gate (heading for Orlando International) and you are waiting and waiting and waiting while little Cindy is screaming "when's it coming?!!" and suddenly the lady on the loud speaker says "Flight 707 to Orlando has been canceled due to a mechanical failure." At that point you already want to pull your hair out. Well, I have a solution. You go up to the lady at the gate and you politely say "I want to pull rule 240!" And at that time, you will be redirected to the next available flight. So you ask, "What is rule 240?" Rule 240 generally states that if your flight is canceled, you can be transferred to the next available flight, even if that flight is not on the airline you originally booked. For example, your reservation is for Delta. Well Delta canceled so you say I want to pull rule 240. The lady finds out that the next available flight is with US Airways. You will be directed to their gate and wait for departure. How handy is that? [Editor's Note: Call your airline for their official "rule 240" statement before you fly and bring it with you. Some airlines will only apply this rule to delays that are absolutely the airline's fault, such as mechanical delays. They do not apply to what the airlines call "force majeure" events: weather, strikes, "acts of God," or other occurrences that the airlines say they cannot control. Also note that this is a U.S. rule and does not apply to airlines outside of the U.S. Get more information on this rule at http://airtravel.about.com/cs/delays/a/rule240.htm]
By PassPorter reader Kristin G.

» Watch for Airfare Deals

A lot of people will tell you to make your plane reservation first then book your Disney trip. We did just the opposite. We booked our trip 6 months in advance and then watched for great fares. We knew that we could change our room reservation to accommodate any special restrictions by the airlines. Doing this saved us over $500 on airfare, with this savings we added an additional day on to our trip and still saved $200.
By PassPorter reader Lori M.

» Book an Early Flight and Relax

If traveling in the winter, book the earliest flight possible! Thank goodness we did this because there was bad weather and our flight was delayed 10 hours. We were bumped to the next flight and those people were bumped and so on. We were the first ones to head out of the airport. We ended up arriving at the hotel at 2:00 am, but if we had been on a later flight we would have been bumped to a much later flight and missed our first morning in Walt Disney World and paid for a night we were not even there!
By PassPorter reader Liz M.

Traveling Tips (continued)

» Drivers Are a Wealth of Information

We find traveling during our Disney Vacation to be informative periods of our vacation. I think that's one reason we never rent a car. We talk to everyone, whether it be bus drivers, taxi drivers, monorail operators, boat captains, or limo drivers! The information that we have gathered from these individuals is astonishing! Many of them have great inside tips on what to see, when to see it, and what to avoid. They have provided us with many interesting facts about the workings of Walt Disney World. We have not been steered wrong yet. Transportation within the "World" can be fascinating if you want it to be!
By PassPorter reader Charissa Z.

» Town Cars Can Save You Time

If you are flying to Orlando be sure to check out ground transportation options. For our family we saved $10 by using a town car service versus Mears. An added bonus was were taken directly to our hotel (no stops at other hotels) and we were able to pick what time we wanted to return to the airport. [Editor's Note: Disney's Magical Express is free and thus cheaper than a town car, but it's still true that town cars will save you time!]
By PassPorter reader Cindy W.

» Use Disney's Transportation

Leave the car at home and use Disney's excellent public transportation system. Learn about where the buses, monorails, and ferries stop, and their operating schedules. This makes getting around a whole lot easier and convenient.
By PassPorter reader James P.

© MediaMarx, Inc.

» Car Rentals Can Be Affordable

Sometimes renting a car for a week can be only a little more than paying for transportation to and from the airport. You can call 1-888-2DISNEY for a discount at National Car Rental. It's possible to get great deals during the winter months. Also, be sure the rental company has a desk inside the terminal to avoid lengthy shuttle rides!
By PassPorter reader Vicki L.

» An Invite to the Antenna Ball

Collect those free antenna balls! We get some from fast food restaurants and our local zoo gave us some "cheetahs" at the last member function. We keep ours wrapped up and let our young daughter unwrap one at the rental car desk (or at the end of the plane trip if she needs a distraction). Then when we get to the rental car, she puts the antenna ball on first thing. It lets her do "her part" and it also makes the rental car easier to find in the parking areas. We even make it a game. "I don't see Jack! Do YOU see Jack?"
By PassPorter reader Alicia C.

= money-saver   = time-saver   = magic-maker   = kid-friendly

Traveling Tips (continued)

» Keep Hydrated with a Camelbak

Be the envy of everyone at Disney. Instead of buying drinks in the parks, buy a Camelbak or similar hydration system beforehand. A Camelbak is a backpack which has a plastic water bag (bladder) located inside with an attached hose and a bite valve to control water. Just fill with ice and water or your favorite sports drink/juice and enjoy all day long. They come in a range of sizes from 40 oz. (around $25-$30) to 100 oz. (about $50 to $80)—the larger ones tend to have more storage space. They are a little pricey but you can also use them to rollerblade or bike. We use them every time we go and everyone whispers about us when they see them. You can get them at sporting good stores. We have definitely paid for ours in our trips to Disney considering the price of drinks!
By PassPorter reader Amanda M.

» Freeze Washcloths For Hot Days

Here's a great way to stay cool: freeze washcloths in a small, resealable bag. Keep the bag in the small freezer section of the refrigerator in your hotel room or buried in the ice in your ice bucket (refill when you can). Bring a soft, small cooler and pack the washcloths and frozen water bottles and go to the parks! You'll love that cold washcloth when you're in line on a hot day!
By PassPorter reader Terry M.

» Get Transparent Backpacks

I bought my children see-through backpacks to bring to the parks each day. We zipped right through the security check points at the gates. And there was no problem bringing in water or snacks. Also, the children could see all the contents, and find their autograph book, pen, or other item very quickly.
By PassPorter reader Debbi M.

» Walk Cool

Buy a set of gel insoles for your shoes. Every afternoon when you take a break from the parks put your insoles in your refrigerator or cooler (with ice). When you start out for evening touring the cold insoles feel fabulous on hot tired feet! This tip works even better if you have two sets of insoles and you can just swap them out every afternoon and morning.
By PassPorter reader Beth L.

» Bring a Baby Monitor

Bring a baby monitor from home and use it when little ones are sleeping. This lets you take that long-awaited bubble bath, or sleep in the next room of your roomy villa, without over-worrying.
By PassPorter reader Janice B.

Traveling Tips (continued)

» Super Cheap Soft Drinks

We constantly carry a one-liter water bottle with us at Disney. We discovered it was very cost effective to also carry pre-sweetened soft drink packets (such as Kool-Aid or Crystal Light), pre-measured into snack-sized bags. Then when we're in the mood for lemonade, we just fill up the bottle at the next water fountain, pour in the mix, and shake. This sure saved a lot of money—sodas are expensive in the parks. Use this measurement as a guide line: measure 2 tablespoons soft drink mix for each 8 ounces, adjust to suit personal taste preference. 1 liter = 33.8 oz., or approximately 4 1/4 glasses. The kids loved this and are planning on doing this on our next trip.
By PassPorter reader Teresa

» Bring Stain Removers

Stain removers, such as Shout Wipes, are a definite must. Just ask my husband who insisted on eating a grape snow cone in 90 degree weather while wearing a white polo shirt!
By PassPorter reader Missy J.

» Your Cooler Can Be Luggage

Since small refrigerators are still $10/day at Disney's value resorts, we decided to use our cooler as a piece of luggage. Ice was plentiful at the resort, allowing us to store milk, juice, cheese, yogurt, etc. in our room without the extra charge.
By PassPorter reader Dave L.

» Bring a Pocket Breeze

Check out the Pocket Breeze available at places like Wal-Mart and online for about $10. It is a palm-sized, battery-operated fan with water mister. Lots of people had the larger sized bottles which are heavy when filled with water, especially in 90 plus degree weather! Other guests and even cast members were stopping us, and asking where we got these cute fan/water misters! [Editor's Note: I have seen small fan/misters at Disney, but there's no guarantee you'll be able to find one when you need one. So I advise you bring one with you if it important to you.]
By PassPorter reader Tracy S.

» Bring Waist Packs for Kids

Since most of my kids are old enough to be somewhat responsible I have made sure that each one has their own waist pack. In this pack they keep their room key, identification, and a disposable camera so their memories can be shared with us all later. We usually take baseball caps for the characters to autograph and the cap is easily carried on the waist pack's strap.
By PassPorter reader Jeanne C.

= money-saver   = time-saver   = magic-maker   = kid-friendly

Traveling Tips (continued)

» Broken Isn't All Bad

Wear shoes that are already well broken in. You will do more walking and standing than you expect. If possible, start a walking routine before your trip so you'll be accustomed to all the exercise.
By PassPorter reader Diane K.

» Bring Walkie Talkies

Take FRS radios (walkie-talkies) with you. I found out the hard way that these are a wonderful addition to your vacation. What made me decide to take these? When my ten-year-old son wanted to ride Space Mountain and I didn't, I let him go on the ride while I sat out front and waited for him. The problem was it started raining really hard and then lightning kicked in. I was out in the weather and was getting nervous because he hadn't come out yet. Plenty of time had passed but still no Josh. Come to find out he was inside the Tomorrowland Arcade at the exit of the ride waiting for me because he is afraid of lightning. He wasn't about to go out and I was afraid to leave our meeting spot. If we had had those radios I could have simply said, "Stay inside I will meet you at..." We will never go again without them.
By PassPorter reader Tonya S.

» Go Without the Kids

Leave the kids at home with a babysitter or go to Disney World before you have kids! It is a wonderful fun and romantic place for adults to enjoy themselves (it touches the kid in all of us).
By PassPorter reader Anonymous

» Camera Bags as Waist Packs

Buy small camera bags to as your purse/waist pack while you are touring Disney. The camera bags are cheaper than waist packs—you can find them for about $5 at Wal-Mart. They can be worn on belt, around the waist, or over the shoulder. You can fit sunglasses, money, and cards in them!
By PassPorter reader Karen S.

» Save Your Back, Bring a Stroller

Bring your own stroller! It is convenient to rent one at the parks, but that doesn't help much while you're in the airport or on that long hike from the bus stop. Before I brought a stroller, I swear my kids must have filled their pockets with rocks along the way—they'd always fall asleep on the bus at night, and we'd lug them back to the room ... dead weight! You NEED your own stroller! [Editor's Note: If you don't want to bring your stroller from home or simply want a really good quality one, you can rent one from Orlando Stroller Rentals at http://www.orlandostrollerrentals.com which will deliver and pick up the stroller at your resort.]
By PassPorter reader Lisa K.

 = money-saver   = time-saver   = magic-maker   = kid-friendly

Traveling Tips (continued)

» Bags, Bags, Bags

Always carry large resealable bags. They have many uses, including storage for half-finished suckers, wet clothes, and souvenir cups. They are also a great place to store papers/maps when you go on a wet ride.
By PassPorter reader Jean F.

» Wear Matching Shirts

Wear the same bright colored t-shirts to the Disney parks. Not only does this make it easier for parents to keep an eye on the kids, it is also easier for your kids to see you in the crowds. And yes, we did look kind of dorky in our matching lime green shirts but it definitely made things easier.
By PassPorter reader Pam

» Cameras Kids Won't Lose or Break

We get our kids disposable underwater cameras to use at Walt Disney World. They come with a wrist strap and are almost impossible to damage.
By PassPorter reader Pam

» Pack a Survival Bag

Make sure you have a survival bag with wet wipes and snacks. If you fly, keep it on board and in the car. This has saved me a lot of frustrating miles, especially with the kids.
By PassPorter reader Tina W.

» Care Packs

When we go to Disney my mom makes up waist packs for each of us kids (17, 7, and 3). The pack has a slip of paper with our name, parents names, hotel, medical info, and our resort ID card (with charging privileges), in case we're separated.
By PassPorter reader Samantha

» Postage-Paid Film Mailers

Bring postage paid film mailers with you. As you finish off each roll of film or disposable camera seal it up in the mailer and send it out. It might not fit in the hotel slot, but I've handed it to a cast member at the front desk to put in the outgoing mail for me with no problem. It is so much fun to have the photos at home waiting for us after the 'letdown' of having to leave Walt Disney World.
By PassPorter reader Stephanie L.

Traveling Tips (continued)

» Stock Up on Chewing Gum

I always stock up on plenty of chewing gum before my Walt Disney World vacation. Why? Three reasons: 1. Chewing gum works great to relieve ear pressure on the airplane. 2. Chewing gum is not always sold in airports. 3. Chewing gum is definitely not sold on Disney property. So if you like to chew gum, make sure you have an ample supply before you go to the airport or to Walt Disney World!
By PassPorter reader Michelle R.

» Use Water Bottles with Filters

For those of you with a sensitive stomach, try what we did. We purchased water bottles with filters. That way we were able to drink fresh water when we wanted and were able to fill it up wherever we were. This was a better alternative than spending extra time in restrooms because of water unfamiliar to your system. [Editor's Note: Check your local department store for filtered water bottles!]
By PassPorter reader Kim M.

» Bring a Pop Up Laundry Hamper

I just bought a pop-up laundry hamper from Bed, Bath & Beyond for $7.99. It folds flat into a 6" circle (held closed by an elastic band) then pops up into a mesh laundry hamper with a circular opening in the top, two web handles, and a side pocket for the laundry detergent/dryer sheets. I toss this in my suitcase, pop it up when we get in the room, and carry it to the laundry room on the last day. I can start my laundry on my way to the pool, then fold up clean clothes and the hamper for the return trip. My slightly sloppy 16-year-old son is more likely to put his clothes in a hamper than a laundry bag anyway.
By PassPorter reader Kathy F.

» Peace of Mind with Disposable Cameras

We leave the expensive camera and camcorder home and use disposable cameras at the parks. We don't have to worry about theft of our precious camera and the photos were great! Weeks before we left I watched for specials and coupons and bought the disposable cameras for much less than a roll of film. Four cameras (two with a flash) were just enough for our family of three.
By PassPorter reader Dawn A.

Traveling Tips (continued)

» Save Time on Postcards

While preparing for your trip, purchase small mailing labels for your computer printer. Print two or three for each person you or your kids may want to send a postcard or short letter to while on vacation (friends, aunts, uncles, grandparents, teacher, etc.). Also purchase stamps ahead of time. When you are at Disney you can simply purchase postcards or stationary, write your note, peel off and stick on your address label, add a stamp, and you're all set to mail. This way you won't have to worry about forgetting someone's address and it's much neater! For something extra special find a picture or clipart that's Disney related to print next to the address on each label. You can even put a different picture on each label.
By PassPorter reader Dianne G.

» Coordinate Your Colors and Make it Simple

Choose a color theme! When deciding what clothes to pack for my trip, I chose a color theme. For example, on my upcoming trip, the theme is blue and khaki. All of my clothes will be centered around this color theme—so it will make outfits easier to coordinate. By doing this, I limit the number of shoes I take, the number of sweaters/sweatshirts I take, the number of hats I take, etc. This not only lightens my luggage, but allows more space for souvenirs. It also makes it simple to change clothes when the unexpected happens. Should I spill something on a top I am wearing, I just grab another top & it will already match the bottoms I have on.
By PassPorter reader Michelle R.

© MediaMarx, Inc.

» Save on Vacation Clothes

Buy your vacation clothes at the end of the season. Since I like to wear "new clothes" on my vacations, I take advantage of the seasonal sales offered. When shorts, tees, and sandals are on sale be sure to stock up. These items can then be put-away until your upcoming trip to Walt Disney World. You will not only save some money, but you will also have some nice new clothes to wear on your trip.
By PassPorter reader Michelle R.

» Don't Let the Rain Soak You, Bring a Trashbag

For my last Walt Disney World trip, I brought along a spare trash bag. I knew I was traveling during a rainy season and it came in handy during a downpour. By poking a few holes in it, I could slip the shoulder straps of backpack through, cover my pack and keep my stuff dry. It might look ridiculous, but who cares! My stuff was dry!
By PassPorter reader Eric

= money-saver   = time-saver   = magic-maker   = kid-friendly

Traveling Tips (continued)

» Plan for Laundry

Plan ahead for the realities of day to day living while visiting the Mouse. Clothes still get dirty, and while I'm no fan of doing laundry on vacation, I'm even less excited about taking home suitcases full of dirty clothes. An afternoon or eve poolside can double as an opportunity to take care of this detail. Bring along what you need, 'just in case'. (Laundry products in the laundry centers are notoriously expensive.) I place powdered laundry soap in resealable bags (and then use a small plastic shopping bag on the outside of that, for a little extra insurance). You can always find an unused corner of a suitcase that this will fit in. The inside of a shoe works great, too. And now that many companies are coming out with laundry tablets, those will be even less fuss to bring along. I use dryer sheets in my luggage year-round to keep them fresh smelling. This way, I always have an antistatic dryer sheet available when traveling. I also pack a tube of stain pre-treater. This way, I have the option of laundering at my discretion, or just bringing the item home many days later, without worrying that the item will have a permanent stain. Especially important when traveling with small children (or sloppy big ones). I've tried the laundry deal both ways, and let me tell you, it is far easier (and more pleasant) to arrive at home with suitcases of clean clothes simply needing to be put away, rather than becoming a mountain to be dealt with in the laundry room. Plus, then you get a chance to wear those 'favorite shorts' again. And, if one plans on doing laundry, you can pack a whole lot lighter. Even my husband has come to agree with this, having tried it both ways. He who never does laundry at home will do it voluntarily on vacation while relaxing poolside with the kids. When packing up to go home, we just designated a suitcase to hold the dirty clothes, the jammies, and whatever had not been laundered. Makes for a much happier mom at home.
By PassPorter reader Jane C.

» Keep Your Stroller Dry

During our time at Disney's Animal Kingdom it rained for most of the day. When we would park our stroller to see a show or board a ride, the stroller would be left out in the rain in the stroller parking section. Even if we parked it under a tree or spot where we thought the rain wouldn't get to it as much, the cast members would have to move it up to make room for the other strollers. We suggest you bring a heavy poncho put it over the stroller while it is parked.
By PassPorter reader Tammy Y.

» Dress Up

Pack costumes for the children. They will love dressing up and they will get extra attention from the cast members and other visitors. [Editor's Note: I agree! My son has been wearing costumes at Disney since he was an infant and always gets the best comments from others. The photos look very cute, too!]
By PassPorter reader Lisa

SAVE! = money-saver   **Speedy** = time-saver   **Magic** = magic-maker   **Kids** = kid-friendly

Traveling Tips (continued)

» Re-Use Disney Ponchos

Want to use those Disney rain ponchos again? Put them in the clothes dryer for 30 seconds only, remove, and immediately fold into a small square that will fit in a small, resealable bag. You are now ready for your next rainy day or wet attraction!
By PassPorter reader Carole W.

» Wear Your Souvenirs

When traveling to Disney (or anywhere else), the favorite souvenir for my family is T-shirts. So when packing I only pack one complete outfit for the first day. After that I pack only shorts or long pants and wear a T-shirt that I purchased the night before as my souvenir.
By PassPorter reader Barbara M.

» Bring a Stroller Snack Cup

A super-handy gadget that helped us on our trip with a toddler was a two-compartment covered snack cup that clamps on to the stroller. It's sold for $5 at Babies 'R Us and is very small and compact. My daughter loves to open and close the lids and stash her pacifier and snacks where she can get to them on her own. The cup removes easily (but not too easily!) for travel without having to take off the clamp. I just leave it on all the time at home, even in the trunk of the car. I can't tell you how many people have stopped us and asked where they could get one, too.
By PassPorter reader Nicole

» Bring Current Photo of Child

Take a current, wallet-sized school picture of your child(ren) with you on your trip. Keep this in your wallet or other water-proof place that you will have with you at all times. On the back of the picture, record the child's name, age, height, weight, hair and eye color, and identifying information (glasses/contacts, braces, birthmarks, moles, scars, etc). Also record any chronic illness, medication, allergies or disabilities. You'll probably never have to use it, but just in case your child became missing/lost you would have a good picture and detailed information with you to help in the search.
By PassPorter reader Heather B.

» Try Light-Up Shoes

On a recent trip, my 5-year-old daughter wore shoes that light up as you walk. These were great during "scary" rides, as even my 8-year-old son Adam could be heard saying "Kelly, kick your feet," if they became frightened by a ride. They don't really put off enough light to be upsetting to other guests, but the distractibility factor weighed high on my scale!
By PassPorter reader Vicki P.

Traveling Tips (continued)

» How to Skip Security

Security at the parks requires that every bag, no matter how small, must be searched. The lines (and waits), particularly at opening, can be significant. My wife and I wore cargo shorts with big box type pockets on the side. These were big enough to hold tickets, money, lotion, camera, film, sunglasses, and everything else we really needed. The bonus is that your hands are free, you can enjoy the rides, and you are less likely to lose things. [Editor's Note: Like anything security-related, the search policies could change at anytime.]
By PassPorter reader Mike S.

» Bring a Massager

We take along an electric massager to use on our tired tootsies after a day at the park. Came in real handy last year when I was expecting!
By PassPorter reader Sonya R.

» Earplugs are Essential

I cannot stress enough that if you are sharing a room with someone you're not accustomed to, bring earplugs! You can buy some in the hotel gift shop, but you won't usually realize you need them until the gift shop is closed!
By PassPorter reader Amy D.

» Bring Extra Shoes

This is a packing tip: Bring two pair of shoes with you. Alternate them daily, this will decrease your chances of getting a blister, as you won't have the same shoes rubbing the same areas all day, every day. You will also have a spare if one pair gets wet during a rain shower or perhaps on Kali River Rapids!
By PassPorter reader Heidi P.

» Cool Off Little Ones

Purchase clip-on, battery-operated fans, typically sold at Wal-Mart and Target. These little fans are perfect for keeping a hot child cool. I use two fans pointed at my child and one fan on the handle pointed at me. It really helps keep tempers in check.
By PassPorter reader Jill H.

» Extra Hangers and Clothespins

I always pack extra hangers—there are never enough in the hotel closets. Clothespins to use on bathtub clothesline are also very helpful.
By PassPorter reader Joan D.

SAVE! = money-saver　　Speedy = time-saver　　Magic = magic-maker　　Kids = kid-friendly

Traveling Tips (continued)

» Save Sanity and Time Dressing

In packing this trip, I am responsible for six children and three adults. Being the "Mom" in the group, I want the kids to look great and be comfortable at the same time. When left to their own devices, plaids can get mixed with stripes! To solve this problem, I pack gallon-size resealable bags with one complete outfit, underwear, and socks. That way the kids grab a bag and I know they look great, they feel good because they did it themselves, and its quick and easy. Later, the bags are used for dirty and wet clothing. This packs beautifully as well.

By PassPorter reader Jennifer

» Packing Tips for Kids

Make a general list of what you'll need and pack a little each day. This builds the excitement and relieves that last minute packing stress. Let your kids help pack their own suitcases. I know my son loves to pack the special "kids" suitcase we purchased for him a few years ago. It makes him feel important that he has a say in the clothes he will bring along as well as those extra special small toys or a security blanket. Don't forget to take along your pediatrician's phone number as well as a first aid kit, child pain relievers, tissues, wet wipes, antibiotic ointment, etc. A small flashlight to help your little ones through those dark attractions is also helpful.

By PassPorter reader Charissa Z.

© MediaMarx, Inc.

Traveling Tips (continued)

» Knowing What to Pack

Check out what weather conditions will be at time of vacation. Make sure you have the type of clothes, rain gear, etc. Make a list of things to do and pack. Keep the list year-to-year and use what is needed at time of vacation, whether its a summer, winter, spring, or fall vacation. Check off the list when you have packed each item. As years go by you will hopefully have everything needed.
By PassPorter reader Stacey K.

» Extra Suitcase For Return Trip

Pack an extra suitcase with juice boxes and snacks for everyone in your family. When all snacks are done, you have the extra suitcase to bring home all your souvenirs.
By PassPorter reader Christine

» Make Your Own Disney Luggage Tags

To make it easy to spot your luggage at the airport, make some unique luggage tags. Just laminate Disney character pictures and punch a hole with a hole punch on one end! Attach it with one of those plastic tie wraps.
By PassPorter reader Jill J.

» Wash it There

Don't overpack! I did and there was no need. Disney resorts have Laundromats, so bring quarters. I even came home with clean clothes.
By PassPorter reader Kathy F.

» Packing More in Less Space

In the past I always rolled our clothes so that they would stay neat and use less space. Last year I purchased a set of the "Space Bag" packing bags. You fold up your clothes, put them in the bags, and suck out the air with a vacuum cleaner. You can get so much stuff in your suitcases with these! For the trip back if you don't have access to a vacuum cleaner, just roll them to get the air out or kneel on them to flatten them, then zip them up. They are so great and none of your clothes get wrinkled. I used them for the first time on a 10-hour flight to Ireland and everything came out beautifully. You can even put all of your dirty clothes in one of the big ones and you don't have to worry about carrying smelly clothes cause they are sealed until you get home.
By PassPorter reader Patricia C.

Traveling Tips (continued)

» Packing Tip For Lost Luggage

Here's a quick packing tip to "up the odds" of still having a fun trip if your luggage is lost. My husband taught me this trick on our honeymoon, and because they lost one of our suitcases on our way to Barbados, I now swear by it! For those of you who each travel with your own suitcase, pack 1/2 of your clothing, shoes, and makeup in HIS bag and then the other 1/2 of your clothing, shoes, and makeup in your own bag. This way, if one of your pieces were to get lost, you would still each have 1/2 of the items that you packed to bring on your trip. If you were to each pack everything into your own separate bags and if one of them was lost, then that person is completely out of luck and has none of their clothing, shoes, or toiletries at all. Better to both have 1/2 of your stuff than one have all of theirs and the other to have none. I now do the same thing with my three sons. I split their clothing into 1/3's and pack a third of each of their outfits (not of their clothes—with my luck I'd end up with all socks and underwear in one bag, pants in the other, and shirts in the third). This way if even two of their three bags were misplaced, they'd each have a bit of clothing to wear.
By PassPorter reader Martha M.

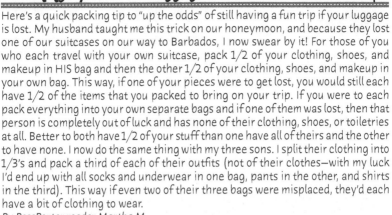

» Pack Less, Stress Less

Don't stress about packing every little minute detail. Our last trip I tried to incorporate every tip into our packing and it ended up being a waste. There is a Wal-Mart about 10-15 minutes from Disney for anything you may need after you get there. They also have merchandise with Disney characters for a lot less price than other souvenir shops! It is well worth the 10-minute trip down there!
By PassPorter reader Jeanna R.

» Start a "Disney" Box

We have a "Disney Box" in our living room. It's a clear, large storage box. In it, we start putting things we will need but won't use while we are waiting to go. (i.e. two way radios, bathing suits, first aid kit (we keep two), extra shampoo, conditioner, etc).
By PassPorter reader Charlotte H.

SAVE! = money-saver   **Speedy** = time-saver   **Magic** = magic-maker   **Kids** = kid-friendly

Lodging Tips

» Reserve Your Resort ASAP

Decide on your resort and get reservations as soon as possible. You can never do this too early! You can always obtain discounts later on your present reservation but your desired resort/room may not be available if you wait.
By PassPorter reader Diana H.

» Florida Residents Can Save

If you're a Florida resident (with proof of residency), you may have special deals and discounts on Disney resort hotels. To find out, call Disney at 407-WDISNEY or visit MouseSavers.com at http://www.mousesavers.com.
By PassPorter reader Allison C.

» Choose a Themed Resort

When choosing the resort we want to stay at our whole family gets in the act! We all think of a place we would like to go that is "not" at Walt Disney World. We would then pick a resort that is most like our other dream vacation. If we think New Orleans then we go to Port Orleans. If we want tropical then Caribbean Beach. For Hawaii, try the Polynesian. This year we are taking an African safari to the Animal Kingdom Lodge. Walt Disney World meets then need of our whole family, rides, thrills, entertainment, and relaxation. Choosing a themed resort helps round out our trip, giving us a different flavor each time.
By PassPorter reader Susan R.

» Check For Discounts

Check MouseSavers.com (http://www.mousesavers.com) periodically for room discounts. If one is available, call and change your reservation over to the discount code. We saved $650 by doing this one year!
By PassPorter reader Elizabeth

» Deals with Annual Passes

While the annual pass discounts on Disney resort hotels aren't as good as in the past, there are still some deals to be had. Keep in mind, however, that annual passes discounts require 60 day advance purchase and a nonrefundable deposit. You also have to have your annual pass (or voucher) in hand when you attempt to get a discounted room. Additionally, these discounts are now only available online at http://www.disneyworld.com/passholders. [Editor's Note: I was recently able to use my annual pass to get the lowest price (that I could find) on an available room at Disney property.]
By PassPorter reader Lyn A.

= money-saver   = time-saver   = magic-maker   = kid-friendly

Lodging Tips (continued)

» Pick Your Resort Wisely

As far as I'm concerned, there are two keys to a magical Disney resort stay. The first is to choose a hotel that suits your family's style. If you have older kids, maybe the Animal Kingdom Lodge would be your best bet. If your family is the outdoors type, the Wilderness Lodge or even Fort Wilderness Campground might suit you best. For young couples, the Yacht & Beach club; for older couples, the Grand Floridian. My brother-in-law recently took his children (ages 8 & 10) to Walt Disney World and forked out big bucks for the Contemporary, but when his kids came to our house and saw pictures of our All-Stars Movies room ($59 a night in Buzz Lightyear) they said, "Oh, man, you guys were lucky—you stayed in the coolest place ever!" So first choose a resort that fits your party. Second, and this is the biggie, MAKE SOME ACTUAL TIME TO SPEND AT YOUR RESORT—swim, shop, eat, play in the arcade, ride the monorail or ferry just for the fun of it, play on the playground, sleep late, go to a character meal (no, your kids are NEVER too old for this!), visit Downtown Disney, play golf, rent a paddle boat, etc. If you're traveling without children, go anytime after Thanksgiving and then "resort hop" to see all the gorgeous Christmas decorations! Whatever resort you choose will have a vast array of entertaining things to do! So, no matter what your length of stay, take some time in the middle of your trip for one "day off," or maybe just do half-days in the theme parks and seriously plan some "time out" to enjoy all the magic your favorite resort has to offer!
By PassPorter reader Stephanie R.

» Pay It Off Before You Go

After you pay your room deposit, pay off the balance of your vacation in easy-on-your-budget payments every few weeks or months (depending on how much time and money you have). We like to send a little extra with the last payment and have a CREDIT on our account upon arrival for charging to the room. Sort of gives us a "cushion" for unexpected food clothing or souvenir expenses.
By PassPorter reader Diana H.

» Hopping Down the Resort Trail

Everyone's heard of park hopping; I enjoy "resort hopping." Even though I've always had a car and moved my own luggage, Disney resorts will move your luggage from resort to resort. This can even be done while you're enjoying the parks. I first plan my itinerary and then plan where I want to stay. For example for Downtown Disney, I'll be at Port Orleans. For the Magic Kingdom part of my vacation I'll move to a Magic Kingdom resort. For Disney's Hollywood Studios and Epcot, I'll stay at BoardWalk or Beach Club/Yacht Club. The different resorts add to the enjoyment for those who enjoy the resorts as much as me.
By PassPorter reader Kathy Jahr

» How Much Time?

You probably won't spend that much time at the hotel so don't spend the extra money for a fancy resort. You are better off using the money to extend your trip!
By PassPorter reader Tara E.

= money-saver   = time-saver   = magic-maker   = kid-friendly

Lodging Tips (continued)

» Stay in Two Resorts

Can't decide which Disney resort to stay in? Choose two. Switch part-way into your stay and Disney will take care of transferring your luggage from one Disney resort to another.
By PassPorter reader Diane Kelley

» Explore Hotels Before Check-In

Make reservations at several hotels in advance. Travel there before check-in, explore the hotels, and stay at the best one for your needs. Don't forget to cancel your reservations at the others early enough to get your deposit back.
By PassPorter reader Edith Elwick

» Request the Best Building

Check the Internet for maps that indicate the best resort building to request. Some buildings are far from the bus stops or the main building. Caribbean Beach Resort is a good example of this. [Editor's Note: If you have a copy of *PassPorter's Walt Disney World* guidebook, it also has maps for all the Disney resorts.]
By PassPorter reader Nicole Laliberte

» Call and Call Again

Try calling Disney Reservations more than once to get the resort you want. You will tend to get slightly different rates.
By PassPorter reader Leanna

» Try Package Deals

Take advantage of the package deals offered by Disney. We found the recent packages to be a great value. Besides park admissions, packages often include meals and other perks. Excellent value for the money!
By PassPorter reader Jasmine

» US Military Has Many Perks   SAVE!

If a member of your family is or was in the U.S. military, or works for the military, try Shades of Green. It has inexpensive huge rooms right on Disney property with all the privileges, very inexpensive Stars and Stripes Passes for every park while you are there, and breakfast and supper buffets. You can eat lunch in the parks at all the great restaurants without paying dinner prices!
By PassPorter reader Shannon

» Off Season Values   SAVE!

Check for special packages, especially at slower times of year. We booked the Fall Fantasy package on year, which included a character or resort breakfast each day along with park passes, for less than it would cost just for our room and park passes.
By PassPorter reader Melissa L.

= money-saver   = time-saver   = magic-maker   = kid-friendly

Lodging Tips (continued)

» Visit Disney Resorts During the Holidays

If you have time during the holidays visit the resort hotels. They are all decked out for the holiday season. It's a great way to begin/end a Disney day. Use the monorail/bus system to get to the resorts is the best way to get to enjoy all that special holiday magic.
By PassPorter reader Dania D.

» Connecting Rooms for Large Families

For a family of more than two children, get connecting rooms with interior door between the rooms at a value or moderate resort. Use one of the rooms for meals—parent's room is the best choice. The other room is the room for afternoon relaxation for the kids or watching TV. Keep the one room reserved for sleeping and eating. It is easier to maintain the room and cuts down on clutter, misplaced gameboys, clothing etc. It is a more economical way to accommodate the larger family than the Disney Vacation Club resort hotel options.
By PassPorter reader Karen B.

» Getting the Most out of Packages

I like the convenience of the Disney resort packages. The only time I felt that I didn't get my money's worth was the last day of my trip because we head for home early in the morning. I finally caught on! Now I book a "hotel room only" for the last night. The park ticket from the package deal gives me addition until midnight the day before I actually leave so I don't miss a Disney moment. I just don't pay the price for being an early bird when I want be needing park time anyway.
By PassPorter reader Cynthia O.

» Concierge Level is Worth the Money

Even though Concierge level rooms are more expensive, we find that being able to get breakfast and bring it back to our room while everyone is getting ready is a real timesaver. In addition, the evening snacks are always delicious and make bedtime a treat. We also make sure we have bottled water, soda, and especially milk in our room's refrigerator at all times! (These items are available upon request at no extra charge from the Concierge Lounge.) We really believe that the expense evens out, because we aren't wasting time sitting down for a big breakfast or grabbing something less desirable just to get on with our day. The food is always delicious, beautifully and imaginatively presented, and available throughout the day. A separate children's area has sandwiches and more "kid-friendly" items in the Lounge. Every announcement that we are going to Disney World is met with "Are we staying on the Concierge Level?" Our kids aren't spoiled, they just know a good thing when they've tasted it!
By PassPorter reader Melissa S.

= money-saver   = time-saver   = magic-maker   = kid-friendly

Lodging Tips (continued)

» Schmooze Your Check-In Cast Member

When making your reservation or checking in, schmooze a little with your cast member. Mention for example that this is your 62nd trip (as this is mine) to Disney and you'd like to stay in a certain room, and so on. You'd be surprised. They are more than willing to accommodate you if they are able.
By PassPorter reader Shelley B.

» Time of Year Matters

The time of year dictates what type of lodging I reserve. During the summer months, I will be spending time in the pool and less time in my room, so I choose a resort with great water recreation. During the cooler fall/winter months I choose a resort for it's "things to do" other than swim, since the park hours are shorter and I will be spending more time there.
By PassPorter reader Lori W.

» Don't Overspend on Your Resort Room

My best advice is to stay where you can afford. Don't get over-hyped about fancy deluxe resorts that you cannot afford! Sure it would be nice to try them, but if they are not in the budget, don't run up a huge credit card bill you will later regret, just so you can stay deluxe (or Moderate). Remember, you are in Disney World, enjoying yourself with friends or loved ones, and there are many many people out there who will never get to Disney! So don't agonize over not having them money for a fancier resort, just have a blast with what you can afford (and guilt-free from not spending the money!). If you can afford $400 a night, go for it! $100 a night, go for it! So many people agonize over this!
By PassPorter reader Liz M.

» Move Around Your Favorite Resort

Even if you stay in the same resort every time you go, try a new "village" or "setting" each time you go. This will give you the feeling of a whole new experience each time you return to the World. We have stayed at Caribbean Beach Resort on both of our visits in the last two years, but at a new village each time and we felt like we were at a different resort entirely.
By PassPorter reader Penny D.

» Stay On Property and Check In Early

First, stay on Disney property. There is no reason not to stay at Walt Disney World with all their choices for accommodations. Check in early, as early as possible. Even if your room is not ready you can check you luggage and head off to the parks. These tips might seem very simple, but few people think of them and they really make a difference.
By PassPorter reader Scott K.

= money-saver = time-saver = magic-maker = kid-friendly

Lodging Tips (continued)

» Prepare Alternate Dates

Before I call to make reservations at a Walt Disney World resort, I make sure I have at least three resort choices and at least one set of alternative dates ready. This saves time on the phone with the cast member as well as frustration for myself. *By PassPorter reader Lori W.*

» Concierge Can Save You Money

The last couple times that we went to Walt Disney World, we stayed at the Polynesian in the concierge building. By doing this, it saved us a lot of money on food. They put out a nice continental breakfast, afternoon snacks, evening appetizers (which you can actually make a meal out of), and late evening snacks of sweets and fruit. It also included all the soda, juice, and coffee that you wanted to drink during the day. We found that with three children this helped our budget a lot. We seemed to actually only eat in the parks once during each day we were there. *By PassPorter reader Deb D.*

» Stay in a Monorail Resort

Spend a couple extra dollars and get a room at a hotel on the monorail line. It saves a lot of time and walking, especially after a tired day in the parks. *By PassPorter reader Deb D.*

» Keep Checking Back for Discounts

Not able to get a discount while reserving your onsite hotel stay? Not to fear. If you are planning more than two weeks in advance, don't give up. Take the reservation and then KEEP TRYING with Disney reservations. Often, discounts are published later, especially if you are planning more than a few months in advance. You can always call and grab another reservation that includes the discount (check http://www.mousesavers.com) and cancel the first reservation. Just be sure to check the cancellation policy on your reservation. Happy traveling! *By PassPorter reader Joan D.*

» Redeem Points for Hotels

If you are a frequent business traveler racking up points with top name hotel chains, you can redeem those points for free stays at 3+ star hotels in the Disney area (including some of the Disney World resorts). I traded in 16,000 Starwood points for five free nights at top line hotel just outside the Disney World gate. Depending on your frequent traveler status level, you'll be able to upgrade your room free upon check in. *By PassPorter reader Victoria H.*

= money-saver   = time-saver   = magic-maker   = kid-friendly

Lodging Tips (continued)

» Check Hotel Availability Carefully

If Disney tells you your favorite hotel is booked, try checking availability at different levels spanning your stay. We were told that the Contemporary was not available from Saturday to Saturday, but was available Friday to Friday—sold out Saturday. As PassPorter's books and message boards have indicated, Disney does not offer information, they only answer direct questions. After several calls to Disney reservations, I figured out that there were garden view rooms for Saturday to Friday, and Tower rooms for the last day. We booked garden view for all but the last night and the Tower for the last night. Once there, we asked if we could just stay in the garden view the whole time. They agreed and refunded the difference already paid.
By PassPorter reader Darlene H.

» Concierge For Less

Every year we go to Disney for Thanksgiving. Last year, we decided to spend it at the Yacht Club as we were lucky enough to get a Florida resident rate of $169 instead of $335. Our room was gorgeous! The colors and theming were exquisite, all nautical with blues and whites, fabulous wood decor, and the resort was completely decorated for Christmas! It overlooked the courtyard and the lagoon. The balcony was fantastic! We even got to see a bride being photographed for her wedding. To top it off, we discovered a marvelous way to get pampered equally or better than concierge, and very privately, I might add. It's called room service! For approximately another $30 per day we ordered coffee and danish or bagels in the morning, and tea, crackers, fruits and cheese at night before retiring. No having to get dressed or get out of bed before having our morning coffee, and being able to relax with a wonderful cup of tea at night before bed on our balcony was sheer luxury! All this for under $200 per night! Concierge on the other hand, costs upwards of $550 or more! I might add that room service is open 24 hours a day, too.
By PassPorter reader Margaret

» Extra Magic Hours are Exceptional!

If you are staying at a Disney Resort, take advantage of the special Extra Magic Hours you receive as a guest. Extra Magic Hours allow you to enjoy certain parks earlier or later on certain days. Details and schedules are available at http://www.disneyworld.com.
By PassPorter reader Mickey E.

» Alarming Mouse

Request a wake up call if staying at a Disney resort. Mickey Mouse wakes you up with a great good morning!
By PassPorter reader Iliana F.

= money-saver   = time-saver   = magic-maker   = kid-friendly

Lodging Tips (continued)

» Visit the Resorts

Take an afternoon "off" from theme parks. If you're a Walt Disney World resort guest, go to Port Orleans Riverside and take the complimentary boat to Downtown Disney, get some ice cream, stroll around and then boat back to Port Orleans. This is a wonderful way to relax for both adults and kids.
By PassPorter reader Laura D.

» Request More Amenities

If you're staying at a resort, you don't need to pack your hair dryer or other amenities—you can just request them at the resort. On my last trip, I asked for a hair dryer, refrigerator, coffeemaker, iron, and extra hangers—all were delivered in a very timely manner with a smile! (The refrigerator does have a $10/day fee at the value resorts, but the rest were provided at no extra cost!)
By PassPorter reader Cathie C.

» Beware of Calling Charges

Be careful when making long distance calls from the Disney resorts. I was charged $6.27 per minute on a recent trip but was never informed that prices were so high. You may want to use the pay phone in the hotel lobby with a calling card. [Editor's Note: Read the telephone card near your phone carefully. Long distance calls are typically the cost of the call plus a 50% surcharge.]
By PassPorter reader Cynthia C.

» Ship It Down Before You Arrive

It's a little known fact that you can ship things down to your resort before your arrive and pick them up upon check-in. We have a special-needs child and the past two trips to Disney we have shipped down cases of diapers, wipes, and a few other things he needed for the trip. We called the resort (on both occasions it was the Polynesian, this next trip it is the Beach Club) and they will give you a mailing address. All you have to do is put your name and the day you are due to arrive on the package and they will have it ready and waiting. It was so nice not to have to carry diapers, etc. on the plane and it is a lot cheaper to bring them than it is to buy them in Disney. We also shipped along a few boxes of granola bars and cookies in the packages for snacks before breakfast to tide the kids over until our character breakfasts.
By PassPorter reader Lynda M.

» Coloring Books and Hidden Mickey Lists

When checking in at a resort, ask the front desk for any coloring books for children or for a Hidden Mickey list. The front desk usually has something special for children—just for the asking!
By PassPorter reader Art C.

Lodging Tips (continued)

» Resorts Have Bed Rails for Little Ones

The resorts have really nice bed rails. Call Housekeeping when you get to your room and they will bring them. This prevents worries about little ones tumbling out of bed. We even bought one of the bed rails for car travel after using the ones at Disney.
By PassPorter reader Vicki L.

» Bring Your Stuffed Animals

Here's a little magic for the kids. If you leave out any stuffed animals on the beds, some of the resort housekeeping <u>may</u> set them up in cute scenarios when they clean your room. When we got back to our room one evening, Pooh Bear was holding the TV remote and all the other stuffed animals were sitting around with him watching (the TV was on, too). The kids absolutely loved it! [Editor's Note: There's no guarantee that because you bring stuffed animals and leave them out that they'll be creatively arranged at the end of the day, but there's no harm in trying!]
By PassPorter reader Judy R.

» Housekeeping Tip Envelopes

I always bring little envelopes with the day of the week on each to tip the maid each day. I usually give $5 in each envelope. I do this daily instead of at the end of trip in case I don't have the same person everyday. [Editor's Note: Ready-to-print tip envelopes are available at http://www.arwolff.com/heidi.]
By PassPorter reader Debra R.

» Bring Your Own Christmas Tree

If you go around the holidays, take a small Christmas tree with you (complete with lights!) to decorate your room. Sometimes your housekeeper will arrange things under it for you.
By PassPorter reader Pat M.

» Turn Off the Air to Avoid Sore Throats

Turn the air conditioner off, if at all possible, when you go to sleep at night. When I leave it on all night I have a terrible sore throat that I have to live with all the next day! I like to keep the air on just until the time I go to sleep. Then I shut it off and never have problems with being too hot!
By PassPorter reader Erin M.

» Get the Refillable Mug

Make sure you buy the refillable mug at your resort's food court. You can use it as often as you want during your stay and it is great for kids who are always thirsty.
By PassPorter reader Danielle K.

= money-saver   = time-saver   = magic-maker   = kid-friendly

Lodging Tips (continued)

» Soap is Not a Souvenir

Use the soap in your room! It doesn't make a good souvenir and it will never be a collectible item.
By PassPorter reader April O.

» Get a Wheelchair at Your Hotel

If you travel with someone who has trouble walking and needs a wheelchair, borrow it from your Disney hotel rather than renting one each day the park. You don't waste time at the parks getting one and returning it. There is no charge for the chair if you are staying at the hotel and it is so much more convenient. [Editor's Note: You may need to leave a deposit to use the resort's wheelchair, however.]
By PassPorter reader Ruth F.

» Get an Extra Day of Amenities

How to get an extra day of use of resort facilities? We do this each year and it works wonderful for us and our two boys. We stay at the Beach Club (we all love the sand bottom pools) and plan our flight home late in the day. We check out at the normal time, but you can still have use of the pool, etc. for the remainder of the day. I pack a bag with our travel clothes (including plastic bags for wet swim suits) and we swim all day. We then change in their outdoor restrooms and place our wet stuff in an outer pocket on our suitcase. Then it's off to the airport. It's like having an extra day and all we do is relax by the pools and go home feeling refreshed.
By PassPorter reader Gerry P.

» Upgrade Your Lodging

Little things can help a lot in "upgrading" your value resort room or off-site lodgings. In the past, I've done things like have flowers or fruit baskets delivered. On our next trip, I'll do both and bring shower gels and shampoos in fragrances I haven't used before to make the rooms seem more "special."
By PassPorter reader Lisa

» Avoid Pool-View Rooms at All-Stars

If you're staying at the All-Star Resorts and do not have children, your best bet is to stay in a building away from the pool. If staying near the pool you will hear children running by your door all night and loud yelling. If you're elsewhere, you will not hear that and you will get at good night's sleep.
By PassPorter reader Nicole T.

= money-saver   = time-saver   = magic-maker   = kid-friendly

Lodging Tips (continued)

» Keep Your Room Clean! 🅺

We usually have two adjoining rooms at the All Stars for seven persons. Even though the housekeeping staff at Walt Disney World is superb, things can get a bit "messy" with four children and since this is our home away from home for nine days we try to keep the rooms as tidy as possible. Each child is given a "chore" to make the room during non-park time more comfortable. One child will make sure tables are clean for snacks, another will separate dirty towels from clean, another will check daily for belongings under beds and furniture, another is responsible for keeping toiletry items in one area since the staff cannot move items, etc. All is takes is five to ten minutes a day to live in comfort.
By PassPorter reader Barbara A.

» Request a Room Near the Food Court

If you stay at a value or moderate resort, request a room near the food court. My kids, ages 8 and 10, get up every morning and head to the food court for their milk and juice while Mom takes a shower. They are even nice enough to bring back my coffee and it's usually still hot when they return. [Editor's Note: You may need to pay extra for a Preferred Room to get closer to a food court at the value resorts. Preferred Rooms are typically at least $15/night more.]
By PassPorter reader Tami

» Stay On Property 🅼 🅺

Staying in a Disney resort is the only way to see Disney. The value resorts are nice for families. You arrive and become a child again. If you drive you park your car when you arrive and let Disney take care of the rest. Get a pass with park-hopping privileges and you just come and go as you please. Staying on property is great for small kids because you hop on the bus return to your room for a while and your off again. The only way we go now is to stay on property.
By PassPorter reader Cindy

» All-Stars are All-Right

If you are on a budget, don't shy away from the All-Stars. They are clean, comfortable rooms, and if you're spending lots of time in the parks there is no need to waste money on an upgraded room. Kids enjoy the decor and the pools. However, we did not find the food courts to be a good value. McDonalds is near the All-Stars and is a better deal for quick food.
By PassPorter reader Michelle

» Request a Corner Room 🅼

In addition to a non-smoking room, I always request a corner room at resorts that have it. Especially in the smaller rooms (at moderate resorts), the extra window gives the illusion of more space.
By PassPorter reader Duane

= money-saver   = time-saver   = magic-maker   = kid-friendly

Lodging Tips (continued)

» Trundle Beds Accommodate More People

The rooms in the Alligator Bayou section of Port Orleans Riverside have trundle beds. This can save some money if you need to accommodate five people in a room. Or, if your children don't want to sleep together in a double bed, then one gets the bed and the other gets the trundle.
By PassPorter reader Angela

» Taking Breaks

Sometimes we just have to get-away-from the excitement for awhile. One of my favorite places is the sitting area under the BoardWalk Inn's veranda. It's a great place to watch the Friendship boats making their rounds.
By PassPorter reader Bev H.

» Deluxes are Ideal for Young Children

If you can have small children and can afford the price, stay at a deluxe resort in the Magic Kingdom area. That would be Contemporary, Polynesian, or Grand Floridian resorts. The ease with which you can bring a toddler back to a room to nap or rest and recuperate a bit is well worth the extra money.
By PassPorter reader Tricia

» Room With a View at Wilderness Lodge

If staying at the Wilderness Lodge ask for a Magic Kingdom view. After a long day, you can put the children down to sleep and you and your spouse can spend some nice quiet time on the your balcony. You can either watch the fireworks or, if there aren't any that night, just watch the changing colors of the castle. It's oh so magical, relaxing, and gives you a bit of time to yourselves.
By PassPorter reader Laura

» Watching the Shuttle Launch

Try to book a room at the Wilderness Lodge when the space shuttle is scheduled to go up in the morning. Then ask at check-in to be a Flag Family. Seeing the shuttle launch from the roof is a once in a lifetime experience! [Editor's Note: The chances of getting to be a Flag Family *and* being on the roof at the exact time to see the shuttle launch seem to be an extremely unlikely occurrence … but hey, if you don't try, you can't succeed.]
By PassPorter reader Art C.

SAVE! = money-saver   = time-saver   = magic-maker   Kids = kid-friendly

Lodging Tips (continued)

» Visit the Polynesian Resort Your First Day

The day we arrive, if we're not staying at a "monorail" resort, we head right to the Polynesian Resort. As long as you tell the parking attendant that you are going to the Polynesian for breakfast or lunch, there is no charge. We eat our breakfast or lunch, walk around the beautiful resort (inside and out), look out over the lagoon at the Magic Kingdom, maybe rent some boats, and then top it off with a ride on the monorail. And, of course, we ask them if we can ride in the front cab with the driver. By this time, our family is so pumped up for our next day's visit to the Magic Kingdom that we're lucky if we get any sleep that night.
By PassPorter reader Eric M.

» Getting Around the Epcot Resorts

Keep in mind that the Epcot resorts (BoardWalk, Swan, Dolphin, Yacht and Beach Clubs) are all within walking distance of each other. To take a bus to any of these resorts, you can hop on the first bus going to any of them and get off at the first stop rather than waiting until the bus gets to your final destination. This gives you a good opportunity to stroll through and appreciate the other resorts. Similarly, when taking the boat to the BoardWalk from the Disney's Hollywood Studios park, you can disembark at the Swan/Dolphin and walk which may be faster than waiting for the boat to stop at the Yacht and Beach Clubs before reaching the BoardWalk. (At least, it seemed faster!) [Editor's Note: It can indeed be faster.]
By PassPorter reader Melissa L.

» Get Your Good Night "Kiss"

All deluxe hotels offer evening turndown service, but not automatically. Call or leave a note for housekeeping for turndown service. The wonderful little "good night" poems left on your pillow for turndown are magical (and great for scrapbooking).
By PassPorter reader Beth S.

» Stay at Disney's Animal Kingdom Lodge

With children I recommend staying at Disney's Animal Kingdom Lodge. My 5-year-old with a never-ending attention span was kept busy all day and into the night. Going to look at the animals at feeding time and throughout the day was like staying inside the park itself. Storytime was just what she needed to calm her down before bed. The rooms were spacious and the balcony gave us a little more room for her to play. The zero-entry pool was another plus. No need to have a little one falling in. Disney's Animal Kingdom Lodge was like a park in itself. Quick trips for a snack and a drink were at your fingertips.
By PassPorter reader Carrie P.

Lodging Tips (continued)

» Take Time to Enjoy the Wilderness Lodge

While staying at Wilderness Lodge try to spend some time in the lodge itself. The relaxing atmosphere and wonderful decor helped make our first trip to Walt Disney World so much more "magical." Take the time to enjoy the resort. As my daughter said, "the resort is a vacation in itself."
By PassPorter reader Helen L.

» Contemporary Resort is Convenient

The best trip we ever had was when we stayed at Disney's Contemporary Resort. The reason was for the easy "commute" into the parks. This is an easy stroll into Magic Kingdom's main gate, or a quick ride on the Monorail to Epcot. It made coming back to the room a snap for our afternoon siesta, and a quick return after our lunch and naps. No time wasted in a car or waiting for a bus!
By PassPorter reader Michelle S.

» Teachers Get Discounts at Swan/Dolphin

If you're a teacher, ask if there are any available discounts at the Walt Disney World Swan and Dolphin Resort.
By PassPorter reader Rebecca D.

» Contemporary is Great for Kids

If you have little ones and are planning on spending the majority of your time at the Magic Kingdom, the Contemporary Resort is the place to stay. We stayed in a Tower room, and it definitely saved the day when we hit the "meltdown" point. You just need to hop on the monorail, it's the first stop, go down an escalator and up and elevator and you're there! You're back in your room before the monorail even gets to the next stop and with minimal walking. It is the best and quickest way to get out of the park and rest up for later!
By PassPorter reader Jeff

» Cook Meals, Save Money

Get a hotel room with a kitchen, it will save you and your family a great deal of money when you cook.
By PassPorter reader Melanie B.

= money-saver   = time-saver   = magic-maker   = kid-friendly

Lodging Tips (continued)

» Old Key West is Better Than OK

The best place we have ever stayed is Old Key West (we call it "home"). With two adults and three children (plus a 17-yr old niece this year) there aren't many places that we can stay altogether in one room (except at the Port Orleans with a Trundle Bed). We have lots of room at Old Key West, can put the kids to bed and stay up late without worrying about waking them. We have a full kitchen so we usually have an early, light breakfast (cereal or eggs) in the villa and do a park character breakfast for the last seating. There is also a whirlpool tub at Old Key West and the kids love that! The Key West theme is wonderful. Such a nice, quiet place to stay. The transportation via the buses provides direct transportation to all the parks. We also saved $$$ by going during a promotion! Keep calling back prior to your trip to see if any new promotions have been applied to your resort to save even more. [Editor's Note: Good deals can often be found at Old Key West, which is also one of my favorites... and it has the largest rooms on property. Note, however, that the studio villas do not have whirlpool tubs.]
By PassPorter reader Deb

» Save Money on Lodging with DVC Points

One of the low-cost ways to stay "on property" is to rent someone's Disney Vacation Club points. I have done this several times at Old Key West for much less than the rate I would have gotten calling Disney. I visit http://www.disboards.com, where I've found people interested in renting points. [Editor's Note: If you want to try this, make sure you understand the Disney Vacation Club point system first. When you find someone you'd like to rent points from, ask for references. Then use PayPal (and their buyer protection program) for the purchase.]
By PassPorter reader Dennis T.

» Fort Wilderness is Fantastic

I suggest everyone stay at the Fort Wilderness Campground at least one time. What can be better than camping out while on your vacation? You have two swimming pools, tennis, basketball, boats, fishing, bikes, arcade, two general stores, boat and bus transportation directly to your campsite, great food, horseback riding, exercise trails, and all kinds of wildlife that come right to your feet begging for food. There is also a campfire show with Chip and Dale where you can watch one of many great Disney animated movies each and every night. What more could you really ask for? Not to mention that you're surrounded by all the theme parks and within minutes from each of them. So rough it out and grab a tent or a camper and enjoy the great outdoors and some fresh air and wildlife. Come to Fort Wilderness Campground and sit back in one of the rocking chairs on the porch, grab a cup of coffee and a newspaper, and let the kids play on the playground.
By PassPorter reader Matt S.

© MediaMarx, Inc.

 = money-saver   = time-saver   = magic-maker   = kid-friendly

Lodging Tips (continued)

» Fort Wilderness Cabins

We have children so our favorite place to stay at Walt Disney World is a Fort Wilderness Cabin. We could cook every meal if we chose to. I have an 8, 10, and a 6-month old, so it is worth being able to go back to the cabin, unwind, and make sure that everyone gets their meals without skipping them because they were too excited.
By PassPorter reader Cheryl B.

» Fort Wilderness During Busy Periods

If staying in one of the cabins or trailers at Fort Wilderness during a busy period (such as a school vacation week), request a site fairly close to a bus stop. It can take 15 minutes or more sometimes for a bus to show up and then it has to go around the resort. Also make sure you get a copy of the Transportation Guide, showing which bus goes where. Otherwise you can end up riding around Fort Wilderness forever before you get to where you really want to go.
By PassPorter reader Ann Marie

» Relax at Fort Wilderness

One of the things that has helped our family enjoy Walt Disney World more is to spend time relaxing at Fort Wilderness. We enjoy exploring the barn and walking along the nature trail from Fort Wilderness to the Wilderness Lodge. The walk is largely paved, level, and takes about a half hour. It can be very relaxing. Although, at dusk, the armadillos in the brush can sound ferocious!
By PassPorter reader Debra G.

» Camp at Fort Wilderness

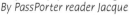

I am not a big camping fan, but our first trip to Disney World was in a pop-up tent trailer. We stayed at the Fort Wilderness campgrounds. After some not too pleasant campground experiences on our way to Florida from Oklahoma, I wasn't sure about spending a week at Fort Wilderness. What a wonderful surprise it turned out to be! The campgrounds were immaculate. Each trailer space was separated from the neighboring trailers by trees and shrubs, it was almost like being there alone. And, best of all, the bathroom facilities were air-conditioned! This was a great blessing in the middle of a July heat wave. I also could not believe how clean the bathrooms were. I'm not sure how often the cast members cleaned them, but I never saw a mess, no matter what time of the day we were there. If you are a camper, or have access to a camping trailer, the Fort Wilderness campgrounds are an inexpensive way to enjoy all the magic of Walt Disney World!
By PassPorter reader Jacque

 = money-saver   = time-saver   = magic-maker   = kid-friendly

Lodging Tips (continued)

» Investigate Off-Property Hotels

When saying off property, be sure to ask the age of the hotel and/or when the last renovation took place. Don't be fooled by glossy brochures or flashy web sites. When it comes to hotels around resort areas like Disney, the price you pay may not necessarily represent the quality of hotel you get. This is especially true around peak times. Also, when staying off property, you need to consider the added logistics time of driving to and from the parks. We've experienced travel times of an hour to and from Disney during peak times and we were only 10-15 miles away. These are things to consider!

By PassPorter reader Gene

» Consider a Timeshare Tryout

Try to book a week at a timeshare resort at their "Try Us Out" rates. We have done this a number of times for under $300 for seven nights in a two-bedroom unit. The only requirement is to attend a 60-minute sales presentation—look at it as a free buffet breakfast and just state up front that you can will not be buying a unit. A timeshare unit saves a ton of money on food as we can eat at least one meal a day in our unit. Unless we do a character breakfast we feed the kids cereal while we get ready which saves us both time and money. We use our savings on those seven nights to stay at least two or three extra nights at our favorite Disney resort (Beach Club). [Editor's Note: Timeshare sales pitches can be aggressive and difficult for some. See my article on my own experience with a timeshare vacation offer at http://www.passporter.com/articles/timeshareoffers.asp.]

By PassPorter reader Steven B.

» Rent a Vacation Home

Book a rental house with a pool if you have small children. When we took our toddler, it was great because during the afternoon (when we came back from the park) he could take a nap inside and we could relax out at our own private pool. (We also brought our baby monitor from home to hear him). There was room in the rental house for my parents, who also came, so we really saved money. The house was HUGE and beautiful. [Editor's Note: I've had similar results with a rental home. They are surprisingly affordable and oh so roomy. I recommend All Star Vacation Homes at http://www. allstarvacationhomes.com.]

By PassPorter reader Donna S.

© MediaMarx, Inc.

= money-saver   = time-saver   = magic-maker   = kid-friendly

Lodging Tips (continued)

» Check Back for Changes

If you're booking your own hotel off-site, keep checking back to look for changes. Our hotel's prices dropped $24/night from one week to the next, and http://www. lodging.com allowed us to cancel and re-book without paying the cancellation fee! By PassPorter reader Eva G.

» Hotel Plaza Resorts

If you stay at the Hotel Plaza Resorts on Disney property (i.e. the DoubleTree Guest Suites near Downtown Disney), inquire about Extra Magic Hours and bus pass availability. On a past trip, we paid an extra $5 for Extra Magic Hour privileges and bus passes. By PassPorter reader Kevin B.

» Add a Touch of Disney to Your Room

If you're not staying at a resort with Disney theming, add some of your own. Bring Disney themed paper cups for the bathroom and buy the Disney shampoo (by Johnsons & Johnsons) for the kids. Find Disney character window clings for the mirror(s) and window(s). Using some paper plates/bowls/cups in the hotel room for meals? Go to a party store and look for Pooh, Princess, Toy Story, etc party items. Have flowers delivered to your room with Disney character mylar balloons. Pre-buy (on sale, if possible) Disney beanie characters to place on the TV, nightstand, bathroom counter, and window sill. And remember to enjoy your trip, no matter what hotel you selected. By PassPorter reader Wendy

» Rent a House for Large Groups

If you have a large group going to Walt Disney World, consider renting a house. This would be good for clubs or groups of families. My family went with a group of fifteen people, and we paid $100 per person for a private house in Kissimmee with six bedrooms and two bathrooms. We had total use of the home including the enclosed pool, appliances, dinnerware, etc. (The owner of the house had even stocked some food for us!!) It was a much more private setting than a hotel would have been. My favorite memory is of us all staying up late, laughing and telling stories without having to worry about disturbing anyone. By PassPorter reader Natoya

= money-saver   = time-saver   = magic-maker   = kid-friendly

Lodging Tips (continued)
» Search for Affordable Lodging

When we realized we were going to Disney I started planning the trip VERY early. I went on the Internet and started searching for tips. (This is how I found out about PassPorter.) I also started searching for inexpensive hotel rates. First I found one for $59/night. Another week went by and I found a rate of $49 through some sort of mega reservation site. At this site you had to pay for the stay in advance and I wasn't too hip on that. I just found the number for the hotel and called directly. They quoted a price of $65/night. I told them about the price on the mega site and they said they would match it! After searching periodically, another couple of weeks later I found an Internet special at a comparable hotel for $39/night with full breakfast everyday! These are all nice hotels too, right by Universal. We saved over $130!! The only cheaper option is $29/night at the timeshare sales hotel. But then you have to sit through a hard sell meeting. Sorry but that isn't in my vacation itinerary.
By PassPorter reader Julie F.

» Bring Beanies to the Resorts

Pack your Disney Beanies! And be sure to leave them on your bed when you head to the parks. It has been amazing what the housekeeping cast members have done with our beanies. We had a Splash Mountain scene in our window, complete with a towel bridge/viewing area, and a long line waiting to board. We had a mass viewing of Disney TV by the beanies, perched on the end of the bed and in a chair, complete with headphones and remote control. We have found beanies perched in room decorations, eating snacks at the table, etc. It was a highlight of the day to return to the room to see what the beanies had been up to. (We had this happen at two different on property resorts.) On one trip, the beanies were just becoming popular and our children had about 50 by the time the trip was over. The next trip, they each packed just a couple of favorites. They don't take up much room in a suitcase—stuff them in your shoes or empty spaces. Our children really enjoyed the antics of their beanies while they were away.
By PassPorter reader Teresa

» Bring Your Own Pillowcases

Everyone in our family packs a different colored or patterned pillowcase to slip over the resort pillows. They take up little space in our luggage. Each of us can easily identify our own pillow. You'd be amazed at how those cast pixies like to mix them up while you're away! An added benefit is that the pillows smell like home, which is calming when sleeping in a strange place.
By PassPorter reader Nancy

= money-saver   = time-saver   = magic-maker   = kid-friendly

Lodging Tips (continued)

» Arrive at Your Resort Early

Arrive at your resort as early in the day as possible. We try to get a 7:00 am flight out of New Jersey which gets us into Orlando by 9:30 am. You will have a better chance of getting the room you want and maybe even get an upgrade. And if your room won't be ready for a while, they will hold your luggage so you can start enjoying the magic.
By PassPorter reader Margo V.

» Send Stuffed Animals Ahead

Surprise the kids. Send their favorite stuffed animals ahead to your Walt Disney Resort. The cast members may even arrange them creatively in your room for you!
By PassPorter reader Michelle S.

» Decorate Your Window

I like to decorate our value or moderate resort room window with our Disney things. But my favorite thing is to put our hometown state name in the window. We have had people stop and knock on the door to talk to us—it's so fun to meet different people.
By PassPorter reader Wanda G.

» Read Your Documents

Be sure to read all the information you're given when checking into your Disney hotel. It tells you when special events are happening—like game time for kids or times for the Electrical Water Pageant or tours of the hotel you are staying at.
By PassPorter reader Dottie N.

© MediaMarx, Inc.

= money-saver   = time-saver   = magic-maker   = kid-friendly

Touring Tips

» Split Your Non-Expiring Pass

We always buy four-day park hopping tickets with no expiration. That allows us to use two days on one trip and the remaining days on our next trip. For the "seasoned" Disney traveler, this makes it affordable to take two trips a year.
By PassPorter reader Elliott W.

» Write Down Pass Numbers

Be sure to copy the back of your tickets or at least copy the numbers on the back. This tip "saved" us twice. First time, my daughter left her ticket in the room which we didn't discover until we were at Magic Kingdom's gates. Guest Relations was able to reissue her a ticket until closing because I had her ticket number. Second time, my husband lost his pass with two days left on it. Again, Guest Relations was able to reissue the ticket with the two days and the two pluses. All because I had written down the numbers on the back of the tickets! [Editor's Note: You could also snap a photo with a digital camera or even a cell phone!]
By PassPorter reader Karen J.

» Soak Those Tootsies

After a long day of walking at the parks, a foot soak in the bathtub with warm water and Johnson's Foot Soap really revitalizes your tired achy feet! It comes conveniently in pre-measured packages, easy to pack! [Editor's Note: If you can't find this at your local store, try http://www.drugstore.com.]
By PassPorter reader Molli

» Taming the Scary Potties

On our first trip to Walt Disney World, our 20-month-old just potty-trained daughter was frightened by the toilets that flushed automatically. We had several accidents because she refused to sit on the toilets. I finally realized that holding my hand in front of the sensor would prevent the toilet from flushing until she left the bathroom stall. [Editor's Note: Some parents also find a little Post-It note over the sensor works if they are unable to keep their hand in that position. Just be sure to remove the Post-It note when you are done.]
By PassPorter reader Sherry

= money-saver   = time-saver   = magic-maker   = kid-friendly

Touring Tips (continued)

» Baby Centers Rule

If you are pregnant, nursing, or with a baby or toddler, check out the Baby Center in each of Disney's theme parks. They are cool, relaxing (rocking chairs), and have cold water and huge changing tables (with something for the child to look at in the process). Especially on a hot day in Animal Kingdom, the Baby Center is wonderful! It was my husband's favorite part of Animal Kingdom on our May trip with a nine-month old! [Editor's Note: I concur! You can also buy baby essentials at the Baby Center as well as feed your baby in high chairs. Other than purchasing baby items, the Baby Center is a free service.]
By PassPorter reader Alicia C.

» Use Package Delivery

Everyone knows that if you stay at a Disney resort you can have your packages sent to your resort. I found out that anyone can have their packages sent to the front gate of the park for pick up at the end of the day! No more juggling bags, kids, and cameras while you are at shows or on the attractions! [Editor's Note: Just be sure to inquire about this service before the cast member rings up your purchases.]
By PassPorter reader Chris D.

» Renting Strollers

When renting strollers for more than one child, opt for two singles rather than one double stroller. Singles are much easier to maneuver through crowds, especially when loaded with large children, and are easier to park outside of attractions.
By PassPorter reader Karen F.

» Choose a Meeting Spot

Discuss with members of your group what you will do if you are separated from each other. A pre-designated spot will help in the event that this happens. A few years ago my son and I were separated from my husband outside a ride at closing time. I waited on a bench outside the ride exit thinking my husband would not leave the area without us. He proceeded to the car thinking we would go there. A discussion ahead of time would certainly have helped in our situation!
By PassPorter reader Shelley C.

» Use Creativity in Travel

Sometimes the Disney buses that shuttle you back and forth between the parks can take a long time. Just remember that you can often travel between the parks if you use a more creative travel method. For example, you're at the Magic Kingdom and you want to get to Disney's Hollywood Studios—take the monorail to Epcot, walk over to the BoardWalk, and board the Friendship boat. Quite often, combining travel with the monorail, ferries, and simple walking can be more pleasant than crowding onto the buses.
By PassPorter reader Kathleen G.

= money-saver   = time-saver   = magic-maker   = kid-friendly

Touring Tips (continued)

» The Solution Is In the Schedule

To see the most in the least amount of time, you have to plan and stick to a schedule. However to relax, you need to slow down the pace. The solution? We followed a strict schedule in the mornings at each park, making sure that we hit all the major attractions in quick fashion. After our midday break, we returned refreshed to the parks and spent the second half of each day touring at a more leisurely pace, seeing the "secondary" attractions and taking in the minutiae.
By PassPorter reader Duane C.

» Plan an Evening at an Early Entry Park

When trying to plan your days, plan at least one evening at the park that had Extra Magic Hour that morning. We were traveling with young kids and did not do Extra Magic Hour but we ended up at Magic Kingdom on Thursday evening (which had Extra Magic Hours that morning). I guess all the young ones came early and finished early because we did 90% of Fantasyland in a little over an hour!
By PassPorter reader Amy M.

» Use Your Own Judgment

Don't skip an attraction/activity based on negative advice! Attractions are designed for the enjoyment of various types people.
By PassPorter reader Ed B.

» Be a Kid Again

No matter if you're 20 or 80 don't be afraid to let the kid in you shine through. I mean this is the time to catch up on all that "lost" time as a kid when you wanted to be older. Go for it—give your favorite character a big hug get wet on the rides, giggle all day, and buy enough stuffed animals to cushion your home!
By PassPorter reader Kelly

» Your First Evening

If you're arriving in the afternoon, make a reservation for a dinner show well in advance and explore the resort or resorts around it. Then travel to Downtown Disney for the evening. In my opinion, nighttime is the best time to visit Downtown Disney. There are many different things to see and do. Can't miss the LEGO store or the World of Disney shop! These both get you in the Disney mood!
By PassPorter reader Donna R.

» Big Groups Should Split Up

If you go with a larger group (more than a couple of adults), don't try to stay together the entire time. Have times to do activities everyone would enjoy and have time to separate as well. There is so much to do—a big group trying to stick together and make everyone happy may make things stressful.
By PassPorter reader Tiffany B.

Touring Tips (continued)

» Swim First, Tour Later

My family goes to Disney every year. As seasoned veterans we have discovered a great way to enjoy the pool and parks without a million other people. Since we always go in the summer, it is crowded! What we do is swim and lay by the pool in the morning until about 11:30 am. By that time, a lot of people are coming back from the parks to eat lunch and cool off in the pool. We go to our room, get cleaned up, and venture to the parks around 1:00 pm. The parks are still busy, but it is amazing how much it has died down. And since we are already relaxed from our morning swim, we seem to be less irritable waiting in those long lines!
By PassPorter reader Angelina C.

» Fickle Florida Weather

Be flexible. The weather in Florida changes hourly. If you planned on a special destination and the weather turns ugly, make sure you have a backup schedule that can be substituted for the original plans.
By PassPorter reader Leesa W.

» Take a Day Off Mid-Week

If you're planning to be in Walt Disney World for at least seven days, be sure to designate one day to "sleep in" mid-week. Have a leisurely lunch or brunch at your resort and meander to one of your favorite parks for a little activity.
By PassPorter reader Denise M.

» Take Your Time Touring

Don't feel the need to rush around. Not all things in the resorts and parks are phenomenal. Take time to plan what you want to see. If you go like mad running around the whole vacation, you will not make it through the week. Go to the pool or water park for part of the day Then visit a park for a while and see what you wish to see. Timing is important. Don't always go to the parks first thing in the morning. Go early a few days. Then visit at lunch time when others leave to eat on a few days. Then after 3:00 pm on other days, when families with young ones are tired out and ready to go home and the park starts to empty, stay through the night. Just remember—there is enough time to see all that you want if you plan ahead!
By PassPorter reader Amy K.

» Slow Down

Don't rush!! You'll end up missing so many of those magical little details when you rush around from ride to ride. [Editor's Note: This may seem like obvious advice, but in fact most visitors do rush and return home exhausted, having missed some of the best things of Walt Disney World. I strongly emphasis this tip!]
By PassPorter reader Faith Z.

SAVE! = money-saver   Speedy = time-saver   Magic = magic-maker   Kids = kid-friendly

Touring Tips (continued)

» Break Up Your Day

Break up each day by visiting a different park in the afternoon to keep the kids' interest high. Tour the morning park until the lines get unreasonable go for a swim at your resort, then head to a different park. It's three experiences in one day!
By PassPorter reader Jerry L.

» Take Time For Yourself

After planning and working hard all year on our Disney plans, my payoff is seeing my family have fun. They ask me questions and I always have the answer, thanks to my planning obsession. My tip to other planning divas is to take some time to yourself at the parks. After about three days into our trip, my family takes a "power ride" tour. Running from ride to ride and park to park to ride all of their favorites again. I go off by myself and it is great. Sometimes I shop Main Street in Magic Kingdom or stroll World Showcase or take in every show at Disney's Hollywood Studios. We only split up for about four hours and meet back with lots to talk about. I even gather info for our next trip!
By PassPorter reader Susan R.

» Tour During Dinner Time

During peak times, many attractions have shorter lines from 4:00 pm to 7:00 pm as most people with children are eating.
By PassPorter reader Sharon T.

» Touring With Kids and Teenagers

When doing any of the parks with a wide range of children (such as ages 4-15), be sure to start in a particular land and finish that entire land before moving on. We have found that doing the attractions in order of their physical location gives a variety between the attractions for the older kids and younger kids. Besides, there are usually several sit down shows along the way which allow the parents a chance to rest our feet!
By PassPorter reader David B.

» Start and End With Your Favorite Park

Visit your favorite park on your first day and last day. That way the last day can be spent in a more relaxed way, leaving time for pictures and memories.
By PassPorter reader Russ H.

= money-saver   = time-saver   = magic-maker   = kid-friendly

Touring Tips (continued)

» Send Someone Ahead for FASTPASS

Here's the best way to avoid lines during crowded times: Show up at opening and decide on the third attraction you expect to ride. Now give everyone's park pass to one person who walks ahead to get FASTPASSes for the group, then comes back to meet you at your first attraction. After you ride and enjoy your first and second rides your time should be up, but first have someone then run ahead to the fourth option and get new FASTPASSes. You can get a new set of FASTPASSes as soon as the initial time appears on the FASTPASS, keep doing this all day and you will be kept from waiting for anything. We went to Walt Disney World for 12 days around the Fourth of July and though the crowds were big we did not wait in line more than 5 minutes the entire trip. *By PassPorter reader Steven B.*

» The Sleepyhead Plan

My tip capitalizes on the fact that our family does not consist of one "morning" person. Planning our early Walt Disney World (Walt Disney World) trips, we were initially dismayed by tip after tip telling us to "be up at the crack of dawn" in order to enjoy a worthwhile day in the parks. However, I am happy to report that being veterans of annual Disney vacations for six years now, we have proven that there is another way! We wake at a leisurely hour and prepare for our day in the park. We will usually get to the park in time to have lunch, or have lunch at our resort before leaving. We then arrive at the park ready to go! Being veterans who have done Disney many times, we know where to go for a cooling break when needed and which rides will have shorter lines and include air conditioning at each park. After only a couple of hours the families that head back to their hotels for naps begin to make a difference in the crowds and length of lines! We usually plan to have our evening meal at the park and again after dinner we are able to outlast those families and tired children who have been at the parks since 7:00 am. We are sometimes amazed at the feeling of having the parks to ourselves even in the midst of the busy season! We always stay until park closing and enjoy the fireworks displays before heading out, tired but not exhausted! Our six and nine year olds have always done well with this schedule and we almost always get to see everything on our trip list! We just returned from our second July trip where we served as tour guides for my sister and she and I both agreed that their first trip was much more relaxing and enjoyable than was my family's, in part because of "The Sleepyhead Plan"! *By PassPorter reader Nan*

» Extra Magic Hour Tips

Stay at an on-site resort so you can do Extra Magic Hour in the morning. Get to the early entry park 20 minutes before it opens and head straight to the most popular rides. Do them twice if you really like them (you will not have to stand in line long) but not more than three times because the park will start to get crowded and you want to get on all of them. At noon, leave that park and go to another park that has no Extra Magic Hours that day. Do the less popular rides at your second park. We did this last year and NEVER STOOD IN ANY LINES! I was amazed! By following this simple rule we did everything we wanted to do and never got frustrated by crowds or lines. It was a very fun-filled but also relaxing vacation! *By PassPorter reader Jennifer T.*

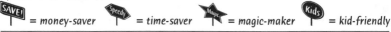

SAVE! = money-saver   = time-saver   = magic-maker   **Kids** = kid-friendly

Touring Tips (continued)

» Plan Late Nights With Care

The parks close at different times and I've found that it's best to plan late nights only every other day. For instance, we never visit Epcot two days in a row. Disney's Animal Kingdom and the water parks make good short days and the rest of the parks are usually much longer days.
By PassPorter reader Lynn

» Free Drinks

When visiting the theme parks, ask for ice water from the vendors. It's not only more refreshing, it's free.
By PassPorter reader Gina M.

» Keeping Your Cool

We always visit Walt Disney World in the month of August when the temperature is most always in the low 90s. After we buy our hats, we will periodically stop in a restroom, wet a paper towel, place it on our forehead, and then put our hats back on. No one can see the paper towel and it sure does help keep you cool!
By PassPorter reader Rich R.

» Remember Your Kids

If you are traveling with small children, take a minute and jot down what they are wearing in your PassPorter before you set out for the day. It's also a good idea to tuck a clear, current photo of each child in a PassPocket. If you're separated, you'll know exactly what they were wearing and be able to provide a photograph. Even if you don't need that information for an emergency, you'll still find it helpful for sorting through your pictures when you get home!
By PassPorter reader Laura M.

» Break for a Nap

After taking five trips to Walt Disney World, I would have to say the best idea we have is to take a nap. My daughter was two on our first trip and needed a nap, and soon after I realized I did also. We get up early, do our thing, and come back before it gets too hot. We nap, swim in the pool, or just relax. We head out for dinner and usually are fresh enough to see the parks close.
By PassPorter reader Corina D.

» Prevent Blisters

Turn your socks inside-out before putting on your walking shoes at Walt Disney World. I can honestly say I have never had a blister since I started doing this! Give it a try! [Editor's Note: Having the smoother side of the sock against your foot reduces friction, and it may make your shoes fit tighter, thereby preventing moving and rubbing.]
By PassPorter reader Jeanne S.

= money-saver   = time-saver   = magic-maker   = kid-friendly

Touring Tips (continued)

» Resting at the Parks

Scout out those attractions or relaxing rides that make good resting places during your day at the parks. For example, while at Magic Kingdom the Walt Disney World Railroad is the best form of rest. No one will make you get off of the train, so we have actually shut our eyes and done a few laps around the park just to regain our energy. At Epcot, Spaceship Earth is also relaxing, especially since the seats are inclined for most of the ride, making it easy to shut your eyes for a little while. Disney's Hollywood Studios is tough. The Drew Carey Sounds Dangerous attraction might work if you take the headsets off—the theater is pitch black and you can certainly catch some ZZZs. Disney's Animal Kingdom's Conservation Station rainforest sound effects booths can act as the same relaxing spot, too. I am not saying that I go to these parks to sleep. But when I've been running around all day, it's always nice to rest my feet and eyes so I can then close the park that evening! [Editor's Note: I'm fond of The Hall of Presidents at Magic Kingdom and Universe of Energy at Epcot, personally.]
By PassPorter reader Laureen V.

» Reduce Wait Times

Your waits in line can be shorter if you ride during parade times. Another way to reduce waiting time it to move quickly to the back of the park and work your way forward.
By PassPorter reader Donna K.

» Prepaid Cell Phones

On our last trip to Disney World, we used (or tried to use) those handheld two-way radios. We found that there was either an enormous amount of interference or a thousand other people had the same radios and were on the same frequency. It was very frustrating. So what we've done instead is buy those prepaid cellular phones. There is no roaming fee, no interference, and no one else is on the phone beside your party. The cell phones are cheaper than many of the two-way radios. You just simply buy the phone card ranging from 10 to 260 minutes and call the number in to activate it. I have had no problems with these Nokia phones. One less hassle is worth it to me. And besides, the phones can be used even when you are back home unlike the two-way radios. This is the way I'll go from now on. The phones and cards can be bought from any Wal-mart Super Center or Radio Shack.
By PassPorter reader Tammy C.

» Use a Stroller

Use a stroller, even with preschoolers (3-6 year-olds). We don't use ours much in the parks (we park it in front of Dumbo and then do Fantasyland), but it helps get through airports with bags and coats. And in the parks it always has a bag with extra clothes, umbrellas, sunscreen, and anything else we might need but don't want to carry.
By PassPorter reader Teresa S.

= money-saver   = time-saver   = magic-maker   = kid-friendly

Touring Tips (continued)

» Bring Your Own Stroller

If you have a baby or toddler, bring your own umbrella stroller rather than renting! You will save money, save time (one less line), and if your child falls asleep just as you are leaving the park, you do not have to take her (or him) out of the stroller. At the Magic Kingdom or Epcot, just push the stroller onto the monorail and "cruise" until junior awakes. You'll have a relaxing break and s/he'll have a nice nap in a pleasant temperature. Or tour the nearby resorts.
By PassPorter reader Alicia C.

» The Weakest Link

Always remember that you are only as strong as the weakest link in your group chain. If one member wears out, it is best to immediately attend to that member by either taking a rest or helping to arrange their transportation back to the hotel, even if the whole group has to go with them. Otherwise, the weak link will bum out everyone. After the tired/sick/cranky member has been restored, you can return to touring with your enjoyment intact. We learned this the hard way with my husband after many nasty arguments at the rear part of Epcot where his knee and his enthusiasm would both give out at the same time. Now we rent a wheelchair put him on a bus, or even go back to the room with him to let him sleep while we swim in the pool. Later we go back to the park with our marriage and our children's happiness intact.
By PassPorter reader Suzie B.

» Backpacks Are Your Friends

If you are bringing snacks or water bottles into the park, use a backpack. As you empty the backpack during the day, you can fill it with your souvenirs that you know you will buy! The backpack also keeps all your purchases in one place—no need to carry around a dozen bags!
By PassPorter reader Colleen A.

» Protect Your Passes

Keeping track of your Disney ticket/resort key can be a bit nerve-wracking, especially if you're in and out of several parks during the course of the day. I used a couple of the plastic badge protectors that are common name tag holders at business meetings. It's easy to find and stays in place! [Editor's Note: Disney also sells lanyards with plastic sleeves to hold your passes, and PassPorter.com has a more elaborate "passholder" pouch which holds a few additional items.]
By PassPorter reader Mariana

= money-saver   = time-saver   = magic-maker   = kid-friendly

Touring Tips (continued)

» Speeding Up Security Checks

Disney's security procedures slow entry into the park, especially for families carrying backpacks. Each pocket must be opened and inspected by hand at each park entrance—it's quite a time-eater if you have a pass with park hopping privileges. We divide necessary items into individual fanny packs far all in our party, which can be opened very quickly, unzipped, and held open at each park entrance and we sailed though. Our passes were kept in the plastic (and waterproof!) holders that can be purchased at the water parks. There is enough room to hold hotel keycards, money, and even a wallet. People with no packages, handbags, or backpacks are not stopped at all. Sending all your purchases back to the hotel helps, too, as these packages are inspected and take some time, too.
By PassPorter reader Noel P.

» Travel Light

Try to travel light to the park so you can enjoy the rides. Bring a waist pack and plan to carry the following: chewing gum (cannot be purchased at Magic Kingdom), bottled water (can be refilled at the water fountain), sunscreen, money, disposable water-proof camera (for the water rides), pain relievers, small first aid kit, and baby wipes or hand wipes. If you're traveling with a baby or small children, bring the smallest diaper bag you can fit diapers, wipes, a change of clothes, and feeding supplies in. Do not forget the diapers or change of clothes (we've had experience with this one!) [Editor's Note: I always leave the big diaper bag at home in favor of a very small, lightweight nylon bag that holds just the essentials. It really helps!]
By PassPorter reader Michelle A.

» Rent an ECV

I have mobility issues and my tip is to rent an ECV from an outside company. They will deliver to your resort so that you have it for anything you want to do! Very convenient. [Editor's Note: I've had good luck with Care Medical Equipment at http://www.caremedicalequipment.com.]
By PassPorter reader Paula M.

» Try a Polar Water Bottle

We found a great water bottle that keeps water cold all day! It is called the Polar Insulated Sport Bottle. I've seen them on the web. We got ours at a sporting goods store. My son uses it when he plays lacrosse and when he goes biking. Someone else told me they take theirs golfing and it stays cold the entire 18 holes! [Editor's Note: You can purchase these at http://www.amazon.com.]
By PassPorter reader Blossom Z.

SAVE! = money-saver   Speedy = time-saver   Magic = magic-maker   Kids = kid-friendly

Touring Tips (continued)

» Shoes For Rainy Seasons

If your trip is during Florida's rainy season, carry flip flops or water shoes to the parks to change into when the rains start. Once your good walking shoes get wet, it can be difficult to dry them in an air-conditioned resort room and wearing them wet will be inviting blisters.
By PassPorter reader Robin

» Keep Cool With Washcloths

Pack wet washcloths in resealable bags filled with a few ice cubes to use when you are standing in long lines or just walking around the park. When you feel hot, just take out a cold cloth to place on your head or refresh your face. If you use dish towels, they can be placed around your neck and secured with a rubber band.
By PassPorter reader Antionette B.

» Two-Way Radio Tips

When in the parks and using two-way radios, be sure to assign each person a "code name call" before hand. That way, when you radio to "Linda," you won't have 15 people trying to see if it is their Linda! We use catchy phrases such as "Roger Roger Matt, got your ears on?" Sounds corny, but does the trick.
By PassPorter reader Linda S.

» More Stroller Tactics

Strollers are hard to keep up with at Walt Disney World. Sometimes cast members move them, other times inconsiderate guests swipe them. In a two-day period our stroller had been stolen seven times. After brainstorming my sister took the name card out of the stroller, turned it over, and wrote "Snotboogers" on it. While sitting on a nearby bench we saw five different people approach our stroller, read the card, and back away (three of them laughing). Other words we used included: catpee, dogbarf, and eyeballs. When cast members move the strollers it is often hard to find yours especially at night. To make it easier to find I decorate my stroller after dark with light "sticks" and necklaces I purchase at my local savings store around (and especially after) Halloween. I have gotten hundreds of positive comments from other people who couldn't find their stroller in the dark. Using these two tips we have not had to replace a single stroller during our last two visits.
By PassPorter reader Cheryl P.

» How to Stay Dry

We keep an extra large, resealable storage bag and a pair of flip flops in our waist packs, backpacks, or shoulder bag. These items come in very handy on "wet" rides like Kali River Rapids or Splash Mountain. We put our sneakers and socks inside the bag and wear the flip flops on the ride. This way we don't have to have wet feet the rest of the day. The males in our party also wear their swim trunks to the parks as they look like shorts but dry faster.
By PassPorter reader Carol O.

= money-saver   = time-saver   = magic-maker   = kid-friendly

Touring Tips (continued)

» Visit the Polynesian Resort

When leaving the Magic Kingdom, if you find the lines for the monorail and the ferry boats too long, try taking the shuttle boat to the Polynesian. The boat launch is located to the left of the monorail station. It's a short boat ride across the Seven Seas Lagoon. The parking lot and the Ticket and Transportation Center are about a 10-minute walk through this wonderful resort. Just head left and follow the signs. In fact, why not stop for a drink at the bar? Once you visit this magical place, you're going to want to visit the front desk and check in!
By PassPorter reader Kurt G.

» Go Left, My Friend

This tip only works if you are at park opening. We always head off to the left. It seems that most people start off going to the right. In Magic Kingdom they tend to head to Tomorrowland and continue in a counter-clockwise direction. We go left (clockwise). While it is not totally empty we seem to encounter less crowds and therefore less lines. We also do not take off at the rope drop. We let the crowds thin out just a little and again avoid some of the rush. Those that tend to take off at the rope drop (going to the left) do one of two things, head straight for Splash Mountain or stop at Jungle Cruise. So the other attractions are pretty empty. By the time we are done with those (Swiss Family Treehouse and Pirates of the Caribbean), we do Jungle Cruise then on to Splash Mountain (which both have thinned somewhat).
By PassPorter reader April

» Fall for the Hall

In the Magic Kingdom's Exposition Hall (on the right after entering the park), there is a delightful area few people know about. It has several backdrops to take photos with your own camera (such as Snow White and the Seven Dwarfs) and a movie screen constantly playing old Disney cartoons (like "Steamboat Willie"). It's a wonderful place to have some "down time," get out of the heat, and get away from the crowds.
By PassPorter reader Carol B.

» Shortcut Through Adventureland

A quick way to get to Liberty Square in the Magic Kingdom is by way of Adventureland. Cross through near the restrooms between Swiss Family Treehouse and Liberty Tree Tavern. One side is Adventureland and the other side is Liberty Square.
By PassPorter reader Ellen R.

Touring Tips (continued)

» Quick Escape Through the Shops

The best tip I received was directly from a Disney Cast Member at the Magic Kingdom. He saw the look of horror on my face as I discovered the crowd that had gathered for the fireworks (on a Saturday!). We were first-time visitors trying to exit the park with our sleeping two-year-old. He came up and graciously suggested that we go through the gift shops on Main Street. They are all connected so we were able to make it out relatively easily. Plus we had a spectacular view of the fireworks on an quiet ferry boat ride across the lagoon! I'm so thankful for that tip! If anyone is brave enough to attend Magic Kingdom on a Saturday, do not forget this!
By PassPorter reader Stephanie S.

» Take the Train to Mickey

Save time at the Magic Kingdom by getting on the Walt Disney World Railroad train ride. Get off at Toontown Station and walk to Mickey's Country House so you can meet Mickey Mouse. Taking the train gets you there before the crowd. Our wait was just five minutes.
By PassPorter reader Ladonna B.

» Skip the End·Of·Day Crowds

My family use to leave the Magic Kingdom during the fireworks at the end of the day. Talk about scary—you could lose your family in that crowd. Then we got smart. We now sit in the rocking chairs in Frontierland and wait until after the fireworks are over and the crowds were almost gone. Then we leave the park. No more stampede for the monorail or boat!
By PassPorter reader Pamela B.

» See Dumbo First

We went on the Dumbo The Flying Elephant in Fantasyland as soon as we entered the park. This ride tends to have long lines and we missed these lines. This also took us more to the back of the park so we missed out on some of the crowds that rush to the rides close to the entry as well.
By PassPorter reader Lori F.

» Join the Parade!

Watch a parade in the Magic Kingdom (sit close to the start of the parade). When it's over, follow right behind the parade until the end. It's just like you're in the parade yourself! Kids love this!
By PassPorter reader Melinda T.

= money-saver   = time-saver   = magic-maker   = kid-friendly

Touring Tips (continued)

» Sanctuary for Scared Kids

We found on our first trip with our son that he was terrified of fireworks. On our second trip we were hoping that he would have outgrown this. We were not so lucky. He loves to look at them but the noise terrifies him. On our last trip we wanted to be able to take advantage of evening Extra Magic Hours, but were afraid to stay through the fireworks (we don't want to scar him for life). We found The Seas With Nemo & Friends to be our safe haven. We went in just as IllumiNations was beginning, we got to see Turtle Talk with no crowds—nobody was inside touring. We changed him into his pajamas and he fell asleep. After IllumiNations my husband and I got to take turns doing some of the attractions we would have never had the opportunity to do, like Soarin', Mission:SPACE, and Test Track—all with minimal waits—while my son slept comfortable in the stroller. It was truly just a little extra magic.
By PassPorter reader Nicole L.

» Fast Track to Test Track

Try the Single Rider Line at Test Track. As long as you don't mind riding in a separate car from your group, you'll save lots of time by standing in this short, fast line. They use the guests in this line to fill in extra spaces in the ride vehicles.
By PassPorter reader Diane K.

» Don't Rush After IllumiNations

When leaving Epcot after the IllumiNations fireworks display (or even Disney's Hollywood Studio's Fantasmic!), don't rush. Take your time and avoid what becomes a very stressful event, especially if your carrying small children. You may even like to walk through to either the BoardWalk or Yacht and Beach Club and catch a taxi from there.
By PassPorter reader Mark P.

» Kids Love Epcot Passports

My boys, who are 11 and 9, love Epcot. To make the worlds more fun we purchased the Epcot Passport from one of the gift shops. The boys had a blast going to the different countries and having a special message written to them in the different languages. We met some very nice cast members who enjoyed talking to the kids about their country. My oldest son even took his passport to school with him. Epcot may not have as many thrill rides as the other parks but it is just as fun and enjoyable. And it's a great way to teach children that getting to know different cultures and people is just as great an experience as riding a ride!
By PassPorter reader Karon A.

= money-saver   = time-saver   = magic-maker   = kid-friendly

Touring Tips (continued)

» Get a Free Photo

For a great, free souvenir, don't miss the "What If" labs at the end of the Journey Into Your Imagination ride. At any of the numerous computers you can take a digital picture of yourself and then play around with it by adding silly facial features or morphing your face into an animal or flower, etc. It's a lot of fun to play around with and when you're done you can e-mail a copy of your picture home to yourself (or to friends). I just returned from a seven-day visit to Walt Disney World and printed the pictures we made of our three boys.
By PassPorter reader Kris P.

» Bring Sippy Cups to Animal Kingdom

When visiting Disney's Animal Kingdom with young children, be sure to bring some kind of sipper cups with you. No drink lids or straws are provided in the park for the animal's safety.
By PassPorter reader Linda L.

» Tigerrific Tip!

Best time to see the tigers actively playing in Maharajah Jungle Trek at the Animal Kingdom is about 45 minutes before the park closes. They feed the tigers when the park closes so they all move to one area in anticipation and get more animated.
By PassPorter reader Gary H.

» Ship Purchases Home

When shopping at the World of Disney shop in Downtown Disney Marketplace, you are better off buying everything at one time and having it shipped home. This is great especially if you qualify for a discount—you don't pay the FL sales tax plus you get your discount and you still end up saving money even with the shipping charges. The only things I take home with me on my trips are breakables. I have found it much easier to ship, so I don't have to worry about packing the extra goodies.
By PassPorter reader Nadine J.

» Downtown Disney Is More Than a Mall

Don't overlook Downtown Disney as just a shopping area. It's a fabulous place to bring your kids to hang out and play. The LEGO store and the fountains alone offer hours of free play for younger kids, and a scoop of Ghiradelli's ice cream makes the day complete!
By PassPorter reader Sharon C.

= money-saver   = time-saver   = magic-maker   = kid-friendly

Touring Tips (continued)

» Water Parks Are Worth It

Make time for the water parks. They are well worth it and a lot of fun, especially for the kids. Typhoon Lagoon is a blast. The wave pool and the Shark Reef are great. After going to a water park in the morning, we still had plenty of time to go to one of the parks. Bring clothes with you. There are plenty of lockers available at the parks. Most importantly, have fun and relax.
By PassPorter reader Darcey J.

» Take Your Waterproof Camera

Don't forget to take a waterproof disposable camera for the water parks, especially if you plan to swim underwater with the fishes!
By PassPorter reader Patricia C.

» Get Sand Off Feet

When you get all sandy and need to clean up, sprinkle baby powder on the sandy spots and the sand comes right off. You smell nice and fresh, too.
By PassPorter reader Eleanor G.

» Avoid Towel Rentals

Water parks charge for towel rental and that can be costly if there are several of you. We discovered that you can take your resort room towels with you. Just ask the room staff for extra towels and the will gladly comply.
By PassPorter reader Jean Alexander

» Bring Water Shoes

It's a smart idea to bring a pair of lightweight "water" shoes with when traveling in the water areas of the parks. That way regular shoes won't get wet and you can avoid painful blisters and miserable kids.
By PassPorter reader Marianne N.

© MediaMarx, Inc.

Touring Tips (continued)

» Water Park Secret

A little-known secret we discovered for Disney's water parks: Get there early and you might get chosen to be Ski Captain or the Big Kahoona for the day! We experienced both of these privileges, just for asking. Our 9-year old is the daredevil and loves to get wet, so she was the medal-bearing honoree each day. At Typhoon Lagoon, she got to "turn on" the wave pool to open the park. Blizzard Beach required her to go down the Summit Plummet first to open the park. Each provided a medal to wear throughout the day, a refillable mug, towels for the whole party, and locker rental for the day, and a shaded spot reserved just for us. Oh, Typhoon Lagoon gave us two-dozen hot, little donuts, too. What a fun way to round out the water park days! [Editor's Note: Obviously, not everyone can be chosen as Ski Captain or Big Kahoona. But as I understand it, being the first in line to enter the water park (and knowing to ask about this), helps a lot!]
By PassPorter reader Angie O.

» Beyond The Parks

Things to do in "The World" outside of the theme parks: During the day take the boat from Port Orleans and go to Downtown Disney Marketplace and West Side. Or go to the BoardWalk and the Yacht and Beach Club and rent a surrey bike. In the evening, dine at Ohana's at the Polynesian one hour before the Magic Kingdom fireworks—lights dim for the show. Or finish eating and go on the beach to watch the fireworks. East at Whispering Canyon Cafe at the Wilderness Lodge at 8:00 pm. By 9:20, go down to the jetty to watch the Electrical Water Pageant on the water. This can also be seen from the Polynesian, Grand Floridian, and the Contemporary.
By PassPorter reader Margaret

© MediaMarx, Inc.

SAVE! = money-saver   Speedy = time-saver   Magic = magic-maker   Kids = kid-friendly

Dining Tips

» Dine Upon Arrival

We always make an advance dining reservation at the restaurant at our resort (which is usually Olivia's at Old Key West) for the day of our arrival. We time it for about two hours or so after our plane has landed. That gives us time to get the rental car, drive to Disney, and check in. If the room isn't ready yet at least we can sit down and have a good meal—at this point we're famished because the peanuts and soda on the plane at 9:00 am just don't cut it.
By PassPorter reader Kim M.

» Dine In Your Room

If you are only taking a short trip there (for example, a weekend trip of 2–3 nights), you would have more actual park time and extra spending money if you eat a quick breakfast in your room (not room service) instead of at a dining establishment. If you are taking advantage of Extra Magic Hours, you would really have the precious time for attractions instead of eating.
By PassPorter reader Janine R.

» Dining on a Dime

On a budget? Have drinks or dessert at the more expensive restaurants? This will give you the experience of dining at the great themed restaurants Disney offers without breaking the bank. What could be nicer than escaping the heat and eating an authentic dessert at France or drinking a margarita at Mexico?
By PassPorter reader Donia C.

» Stash Your Snacks

Since the food prices are so high at Walt Disney World, I pack a lunch and snacks that do not require refrigeration. I get one of the lockers on the way into the Magic Kingdom and stash it there. We meet back at the lockers for a meal and/or snacks. [Editor's Note: Disney's official policy is that guests may not bring food or beverage items into the park unless it is required for special dietary needs. In practice, however, small amounts of food are usually overlooked. Do not try to bring in big coolers or huge sacks full of food, however.]
By Anonymous

» Relaxing with Room Service

After we get back to the hotel at the end of the day, we like to order the cheese and fruit plate plus milk from room service. While we ate we would talk about what we wanted to do the next day.
By PassPorter reader Samantha

Dining Tips (continued)

» Try Different Dishes

Since the portions at Walt Disney World are so large, we make sure that at least one person orders something we have never had and then we all share it. And if no one likes it, there is plenty for all from the other dishes. This way the kids (and their parents) are exposed to different dishes with no threat of not eating.
By PassPorter reader Teresa S.

» Refillable Mugs Rock

Buy refillable mugs at your resort. We send the first person dressed in the morning for coffee and hot chocolate. The mugs have lids, so spilling hot drinks is not such a problem. Then the rest of us can get dressed in a more leisurely (and better tempered, since we are having our coffee) manner. When the kids are at the pool, they can run back and forth and get their own drinks without me having to hand out money every five minutes. Then at the end of our trip, we have the mugs as nice souvenirs.
By PassPorter reader Sherry G.

» Breakfast in Bed

To surprise my loving husband, I slip out of the room while he's still asleep in the morning, go to our resort's food court, and bring back breakfast. Then we have "breakfast in bed."
By PassPorter reader Darla

» Adventures in Dining

Get out of your comfort zone and try something new! It is hard to resist going back to dine at your favorite places on every trip. A sense of adventure on a recent trip has left me with a whole new list of favorites. I never would have guessed my favorite food at Disney would be African! The flavors of Boma, Mara, and the Tangerine Cafe have me dreaming for more. (I can't wait to try Jiko.) The only drawback to this is that your list of favorites will keep growing and growing. The only solution seems to be planning longer trips you can fit in all the old favorites while leaving room for more adventures in dining.
By PassPorter reader Greta

» Save Money and Pounds

To save money—and keep off the extra weight usually put on during vacations—order only one entree for two people to share. Most restaurants give portion sizes that are almost double what we should be eating in a meal.
By PassPorter reader Mindy G.

= money-saver   = time-saver   = magic-maker   = kid-friendly

Dining Tips (continued)

» Eat In-Room for Early Entry Days

We love to get to the parks early and take advantage of the early entry. So the night before we go to the food court and buy two large drinks (usually juice) and put them in the refrigerator or ice box overnight. We bring a couple boxes of breakfast bars on our trip and have those and the juice in the morning in the room while getting dressed. This way we don't have to get up even earlier . We make lunch and dinner our two big meals and eat at oddball times so we avoid the meal time crowds.
By PassPorter reader Ed E.

» Keep Dining Plans Flexible

Don't set too many meal plans in concrete—be very flexible. We found that due to line waits and distance to travel, all our well-laid plans simply crumble under the pressure. The day we planned to watch the Magic Kingdom parade our intention was to sit down and eat a good lunch at Liberty Tree Tavern around 1:00 pm, but by the time we made it there (closer to 2:00 pm) and factored in the 30-minute wait for a table, ordering time, and eating time, we wouldn't have had a chance at a good viewing spot for the parade so... we actually had brownies and ice cream topped with M&M's for lunch at the Sleepy Hollow snack spot on the edge of Liberty Square. We got our brownies and root beers and sat at the first table (also closest to the bridge) and called that lunch. We finished eating about 20 minutes before the parade but never went in search of a better viewing spot—we wouldn't have found one anyway—it was the perfect spot.
By PassPorter reader Redonna L.

» Check the Menu First

Dining with children can sometimes be a chore. To make your trip more enjoyable be sure to check out the menu before being seated or waiting in line. The choices may sometimes be limited and not include your child's favorites. [Editor's Note: You can also read menus before you leave home at http://www.allears.net.]
By PassPorter reader Lisa M.

» Character Meals Save Time and Money

Choose a character meal or fine dining restaurant once each day. The cost of the character lunches is comparable to that of what you would spend for counter service including drink and snacks. By choosing the character meals you get the best of both worlds, great food, a chance to sit and relax, and not have to fight the crowds to meet and greet the characters. Choose your meals by the characters you want to meet. We chose Crystal Palace first for the Pooh gang, then tasted some great culture at the Teppanyaki Room at Epcot's Japan, and finished our journey by going over to the Grand Floridian after a day at Disney's Animal Kingdom and feasting at 1900 Park Fare. We were able to see all of our favorites and have great food with it!
By PassPorter reader Kelly

= money-saver   = time-saver   = magic-maker   = kid-friendly

Dining Tips (continued)

» Snack in each Country at Epcot

For your day at Epcot take the time to check out the menus from every area, then plan to snack all day versus eating full meals. This allows you to "taste" a little from each country and enjoy the many cultures available there.
By PassPorter reader Kelly

» Chicken or Pizza?

When the parents want a dinner meal like chicken and the kids want pizza, we found it best to do both! First we divided up (to save time) mom and one child get the pizza and meet dad and the other child at the restaurant serving chicken dinner and everyone eats together! Everyone got want they wanted to eat. It was great!
By PassPorter reader Betty C.

» Kids Eat Free at Buffets

Most buffets are free for children under three. We found this to be a big advantage when choosing where to eat. Our picky eater was able to choose what he wanted and we didn't feel bad when he only ate two bites of his meal.
By PassPorter reader Melanie L.

» Plan Out Mealtimes With Kids

Plan your meals in advance. There is nothing worse than being in the Magic Kingdom in 80 degree weather with three hot, hungry children and being unable to find a place to eat with food that all of them will like. Not every child likes hamburgers and hot dogs. Know where the food your family likes is located, and don't wait until your kids are starving before you decide to stop.
By PassPorter reader Kim

» Eat Well and Still Watch Your Budget

I always suggest to those who are watching their budgets to eat lunch in the full-service restaurants around the parks and then have counter-service food for dinner. The lunches are much less expensive in most cases and also easier to get reservations for. That and it can be a nice break from the heat in the middle of the afternoon.
By PassPorter reader Leigh M.

» Ship Your Meals to Your Hotel

We pack a big box full of goodies like paper goods, hot cocoa, Kool-Aid mix, instant oatmeal, cheese and crackers, cereal, granola bars, etc. and ship it to our resort. We use UPS and send it in advance so it is waiting when we check-in. So instead of spending $40 and 45 minutes a day at the food court for breakfast, we eat the inexpensive items we shipped. It worked like a charm! The shipping cost was minimal, the vacation time we saved was enormous.
By PassPorter reader Stephanie R.

Dining Tips (continued)

» Empower Kids at Meals

On our trip to Walt Disney World, we gave our 6-year-old daughter two passes to choose where we eat for a meal. This allowed her to choose a couple of places to eat. If she didn't like a place, we point out that she had the opportunity to choose a few meals, and now it's mommy and daddy's turn to choose. By giving her some passes, it's also a more concrete way of making sure she understands that she was able to make a couple of choices all by herself.
By PassPorter reader Charmaine D.

» No Need to Pay for a Full Meal

Want to experience the dining adventure of the Sci-Fi Dine-In Theater or the '50s Prime Time Cafe without paying for a full meal for everyone in the family? Try going in the mid-afternoon for an ice cream snack. You can cool off with a shake while you watch corny sci-fi flicks or have a Black Cow served by "Mom" at the '50s Prime Time Cafe. (Yum!)
By PassPorter reader Jan

» Snack Around World Showcase

We enjoy dining at each Epcot's World Showcase. Snack your way around the world. Don't order meals—order appetizers instead.
By PassPorter reader Jacque B.

» Easy Bibs for Kids

Be sure to pack at least one plain hair elastic (ponytail holder) or even a rubber band for each small child. When at restaurants, use the elastic to secure their napkin around their neck for an easy bib that stays in place. No more worries about spills!
By PassPorter reader Karen C.

» Order a Pizza in Your Room

Here's a hint for a cheap Disney meal: order pizza to your room. It's perfect for several reasons it's about $20 (MUCH less than most Disney meals), it's something the kids love, and it allows you to rest in the room after a long day of fun at the parks.
By PassPorter reader Theresa

» Staying on Your Diet

One year my husband and I were on a diet when we visited Disney World. We brought along soup packets (dry) and large styrofoam cups. We ordered a salad at one of the fast food restaurants and a cup of hot water. We bought a piece of fruit from one of the stands. We mixed our own soup and had a nice salad and fruit for lunch. For snacks, we brought raisins or crackers and a small jar of peanut butter. None of these items spoil and we managed to actually lose weight while there!
By PassPorter reader Susan B.

= money-saver   = time-saver   = magic-maker   = kid-friendly

Dining Tips (continued)

» Bring Fixins for PB&J Sandwiches

We carry a non-breakable jar of jelly and a couple loaves of bread in a plastic container to make PB&J's in our hotel room. Sometimes we just don't feel like going out to scrounge food, or to rent a refrigerator, or need a quick snack before a later dinner. The sandwiches are a lifesaver. With the money we save on snacks and a few meals, the empty room in the suitcase quickly fills with souvenirs for the ride home! [Editor's Note: Peanut butter and jelly is a particularly good snack because you get quick energy from the sugar in the jelly and energy for later from the protein in the peanut butter. Try it!]
By PassPorter reader Marion C.

» Share and Share Alike

Depending on your trip budget, sharing is always a good thing! Often when we go to the "World" my husband and I will order a few appetizers off a menu to get a good sampling of one of the pricier sit down restaurants in the parks. Other times we will each get something and split our meals so that we both have tried at least two things off the menu in our visit. It gives us a good feel for the offerings, let's us share the food experience, and also helps us not get too much food. While we don't necessarily stick to our diets while on vacation, we don't completely lose sight of our goals! Walt Disney World as many places, is known for its large servings and doggie bags really aren't helpful unless you have a refrigerator and a means of reheating. Unless it's stated on the menu, it's always acceptable (and fun) to share!
By PassPorter reader Pamela R.

» Do the Disney Double Dip

After leaving Disney's Hollywood Studios, take the boat to Epcot to have a great dinner in the World Showcase!
By PassPorter reader Debbie S.

» Get Sunrise/Sunset Times

Download a table that has the sunrise and sunset times. This can help you to decide on when to make your dinner reservations.
By PassPorter reader Jean F.

» Sit Down For a Meal

Schedule a sit-down meal between 2:00 and 4:00 pm. The prices are better and the "rest" will recharge the batteries for the remainder of the day and evening.
By PassPorter reader Linda T.

SAVE! = money-saver   = time-saver   = magic-maker   = kid-friendly

Dining Tips (continued)

» Late Lunch, Early Dinner

To save money on food but still enjoy the nicer restaurants of Walt Disney World, take the last reservation slot for lunch around 3:30 or 4:00. You still can enjoy just about everything on the menu, but at much reduced prices. By doing this you will also miss the lunch and dinner crowds. You can enjoy the rest of the park while everyone else is eating. You'll want a big breakfast to start the day with, of course!
By PassPorter reader Donia C.

» Make it a Late Breakfast

On our last trip to Walt Disney World, we adjusted our breakfast schedule to give us a little more time in the Magic Kingdom. If you're planning a breakfast at the Grand Floridian, Cinderella Castle, or the Contemporary, make your reservations around 10:30 am on day with Extra Magic Hour morning at the Magic Kingdom. Then take advantage of the early entry and spend a couple of hours there before the parks fills up. You can grab something to snack on at the Main Street Bake Shop. Then when it's time, enjoy your sit-down breakfast. After breakfast, when the park has gotten crowded, hop on the monorail and take in Epcot. We've found that this give us more time for doing the rides—the lines are shorter earlier in the morning. And the late breakfast is actually eliminates the need for lunch. It is both a time and money saver.
By PassPorter reader Tim T.

» Make Reservations Before Leaving

I have been to Disney World at Christmas time for the past two years. I have eaten many wonderful places on Disney property, as well as character meals. But I can assure you this... make your advance reservations for restaurants before you leave home, write down your confirmation number, and arrive at least 30 minutes prior to your meal time. You will have smooth results if you prearrange your meals. It is my personal opinion that breakfast meals are the fastest, easiest way to enjoy a character meal. The kids are happy and excited with anticipation and everything seems so fresh and pure Disney magic. But please prearrange your meals at home—you will be seated earlier and spend less time in line!
By PassPorter reader Dawn S.

» Fantasmic Dining Package

Take advantage of Fantasmic Dining Package at Disney's Hollywood Studios. Not only does it give you a reservation for dinner, but it also guarantees a seat for that night's performance of "Fantasmic!" It sure beats having to arrive really early for Fantasmic! [Editor's Note: To reserve this dining package, call 407-WDW-DINE up to 180 days in advance.]
By PassPorter reader Sally K.

= money-saver   = time-saver   = magic-maker   = kid-friendly

Dining Tips (continued)

» Don't Miss Your Reservation

Make reservations for 20-30 minutes after you realistically believe you'll arrive at the restaurant. It's no big deal to be "early" and most of the time you won't wait to be seated any longer than if you had arrived at your scheduled time because the restaurants seem to seat in order of arrival. But if you're running late (we all know about those Disney buses) and you've set a later seating time, you won't lose your reservation... plus you won't feel so stressed!
By PassPorter reader Melissa

» Fast Food, Fast Rides

My sister and I toured the parks together with no kids this past year. We didn't know what we wanted for lunch so we looked around deciding on just the right place. I called the dining number on my cell phone and made reservations while getting a FASTPASS at the same time. We went right from that ride, picked up another FASTPASS, and then went to our lunch reservation. We had no wasted time and enjoyed fast seating in the restaurant, followed by quick entrance to our next attraction
By PassPorter reader Cynthia O.

» Beaches and Cream Penny Pincher

Here's a great way for a family of four to eat cheap at the Yacht & Beach Clubs: Go to Beaches and Cream, order two orders of Burger Heaven, and split them between you and the kids. You get tons of fries and huge burgers for less than $16. Then order one of the great $6 sundaes to split among the four of you, which is more than enough considering how full you will be from the burgers and fries.
By PassPorter reader Steven B.

» Best Pizza in the World

Looking for the best pizza in the "World"? Check out the All-Star Music food court. And if you stay there they will deliver it to your room! Mmm, mmm, good.
By PassPorter reader David Whiteman

» Ask For Recipes

When eating at a Disney restaurant and you find a particular dish that you like, ask for the recipe! We loved the dressing on one of the salads and the honey butter—we made mention of this to our server and at the end of our dinner we were given a photocopy of the two recipes!
By PassPorter reader Lynda M.

= money-saver   = time-saver   = magic-maker   = kid-friendly

Dining Tips (continued)

» Meal Magic

On our last trip to Walt Disney World I had a three-day convention in Orlando before we checked into the Beach Club. It drove us nuts being so close, but not seeing Disney. One evening we drove over to the Grand Floridian and checked at Narcoossees. Since we didn't reservations, we had to wait about 20 minutes. We went out on the patio over the water and had a fabulous view of Magic Kingdom with the castle turning colors every few minutes. Then while looking over the lagoon we noticed that a full moon was rising over the Contemporary. What a beautiful sight. We had a delicious dinner (lobster with vanilla sauce the BEST) and enjoyed our seat by the window overlooking the bay and still watching the castle. After dinner we went around the corner and caught the boat over to Magic Kingdom got off and took the monorail to the Contemporary and went up to the roof to watch the Magic Kingdom fireworks. Spectacular place to view them and they pipe through the music well. After that we took the boat to the Wilderness Lodge, our favorite hotel.
By PassPorter reader Becky K.

» Chill Out at Cosmic Ray's

Cosmic Ray's Starlight Cafe in the Magic Kingdom is an often overlooked gem! For the price of a counter-service meal (excellent Caesar Salad by the way), you can enjoy the ultimate lounge lizard experience. Sunny Eclipse is a space-age cross of Bill Murray and Rodney Dangerfield—don't miss the Small World reference. It's never crowded there. In fact, sometimes we go in just for the show and to beat the heat—you don't even need to buy anything.
By PassPorter reader Susan P.

» Boma is a Bargain!

The dinner buffet at Boma in Disney's Animal Kingdom Lodge is a fantastic bargain at only $31. It's less expensive than dinner at most of the nicer Walt Disney World restaurants. The selection is great! There's something to please all tastes, and the service is attentive without being overly so. Disney's Animal Kingdom Lodge is beautiful at anytime, but especially so in the evening. Also—and here's a real perk—with a reservation at Boma or Jiko, non-Lodge guests may drive onto the property. The only others allowed to bring their vehicles in are those staying at Disney's Animal Kingdom Lodge. I think this could become a tough reservation to get now that word is spreading about just how good the food is here.
By PassPorter reader Susan P.

Dining Tips (continued)

» Celebrating a Birthday at Crystal Palace

My husband Richard's favorite character is Tigger, I guess because they are both very bouncy. Richard is just a big kid. Last year when we went to "the World," it was the week of his birthday. We surprised him with a character lunch at the Crystal Palace, which stars all of the Winnie the Pooh characters. They surprised him with a birthday cupcake complete with candle. The cast members sang to him and completely surprised him. Of course, Tigger paid special attention to him, hugging him several times. We found that getting a reservation for 1:00 pm got us there after the crowd for lunch and we got much more attention then we had expected. The lunch is served buffet-style and it was hot, fresh, and plentiful. We had a wonderful time and he is still talking about it.
By PassPorter reader Patricia C.

» 50s Prime Time Cafe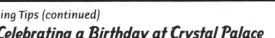

Every year, while touring Disney's Hollywood Studios, we make advance reservations for 50s Prime Time Cafe! We make them early, around 5:00-5:30 pm. Maybe it's my age, growing up in the '50-'60s era, but even my children enjoy it. You are usually seated in a small area with five to seven tables. Upon your arrival at your table, your assigned server refers to you as "cousins" to the other diners in your area. When your meal is served, they check on you constantly to see that you are eating everything on your plate, no elbows on the table etc. This past year my daughter had a chicken tenders dinner with corn on the cob. She did not eat the corn and explained to our waiter that she did not want to get it all stuck in her braces. He promptly took a knife and scraped all the corn OFF the cob and onto her plate and proceeded to spoon feed her. Needless to say she was mortified! After a hilarious dinner we go directly to the Fantasmic show. Even though we could get the Fantasmic Dinner Package at other restaurants at Disney's Hollywood Studios, we just love going back each year to '50s Prime Time Cafe.
By PassPorter reader Debbi T.

» Fireworks During Dinner

Watch the fireworks over Cinderella Castle while having an amazing dinner at the California Grill in the Contemporary Resort.
By PassPorter reader Cindy

» Shake it Up at Restaurant Marrakesh

Restaurant Marrakesh in Morocco is the most overlooked restaurant. It is quiet and usually you don't need a reservation. Food is great and you can find something for everyone. And it seems like everyone loves the belly dancers, both male and female.
By PassPorter reader Jerald M.

Dining Tips (continued)

» San Angel Inn

Get the first reservation time at the San Angel Inn (in Mexico at Epcot) and request to sit by the river. It is so relaxing.
By PassPorter reader Trudy H.

» Columbia Harbour House

One of my favorite eateries is the Columbia Harbour House in Liberty Square at the Magic Kingdom. If you try to eat early (around 11:00 am) you can usually get a table and quick service.
By PassPorter reader Diane

» A Yummy Snack Disney Offers

While in Magic Kingdom or Downtown Disney I like to stop in the candy store and purchase a couple of those wonderful caramel-coated apples! While I enjoy eating one immediately, I have the second apple wrapped to eat as a snack later. For the time between the apples I like to find a quick counter-service restaurant to grab a quick meal. More time to spend out in the real Walt Disney World!
By PassPorter reader Jackie R.

» Be Wary of Murky Waters!

When we travel to Walt Disney World we always enjoy eating at the Coral Reef Restaurant in The Seas with Nemo & Friends at Epcot. However on my last trip when we arrived to eat, there was zero visibility in the Living Seas tank. This was a real disappointment as the whole experience of eating there is centered around the ambiance and the view of the tank. We found out from our waiter that the reason the tank was so cloudy was due to scheduled cleaning. When we arrived at Walt Disney World we called to confirm our reservation and the cast member did not inform us of any visibility issues with the tank nor did the hostess when we arrived. The best tip that I can offer is to inquire about the visibility of the tank, especially if you are traveling during the value seasons, to ensure an enjoyable dining experience at the Coral Reef Restaurant.
By PassPorter reader Adriane F.

» French Bakery Hits the Spot

In Epcot try a little of everything especially the bakery in France (Boulangerie Patisserie)! The line can be long (especially as IllumiNations approaches), but well worth the wait. On a cold winter day hot cocoa and a French pastry hit the spot.
By PassPorter reader Jan C.

= money-saver   = time-saver   = magic-maker   = kid-friendly

Dining Tips (continued)

» Stop for Afternoon Tea

No matter where you're staying, treat yourself to afternoon high tea at the Grand Floridian. There are many delightful selections to choose from, but remember that you can also create your own tea selection by ordering a la carte. After tea, hang out in the plush lobby enjoying the music and the atmosphere. I particularly recommend this high tea for single travelers, couples over 50, and adults celebrating a birthday, anniversary or other special occasion.
By PassPorter reader Mary Beth A.

» Watch Fireworks at Narcoossees

Every year we eat at Narcoossees at the Grand Floridian. We love the food and atmosphere, but what's most important is we make our reservation so that we can eat and then go out to the porches and watch the fireworks from the Magic Kingdom. This is such a great view because the music is piped in and no one is allowed on the porches except Narcoossees' guests. Then we go back and enjoy a nice dessert. What a great way to enjoy the fireworks and avoid the crowds at the Magic Kingdom!
By PassPorter reader Karon A.

» Ask For Ketchup at Whispering Canyon Cafe!

While eating at the Whispering Canyon Cafe in the Wilderness Lodge, be sure to ask for some ketchup. My husband had a big surprise as he ended up with 25 bottles of ketchup delivered by diners from all over the restaurant. But beware—if you try to steal ketchup from another table, the servers will make you do some horrible thing, like ride a hobby horse through the lobby!! [Editor's Note: Your experience at Whispering Canyon Cafe may vary, of course, but they do seem to have a thing about ketchup there!]
By PassPorter reader Shawn K.

» Filling Meal for Less

If you are looking for a cheap and quick meal at Epcot, pay attention to the food stands around the World Showcase. While they tend to change around a bit, especially during the Food & Wine Festival, they can still provide a hearty helping at a reasonable price.
By PassPorter reader Susan

» Visit Olive Garden During Your Stay

We really enjoy eating at the Disney restaurants. We plan our meals prior to leaving home so that we don't feel too "stuffed" to eat one more good meal. And to help with the expense, we buy an Olive Garden gift card before leaving home. In the middle of the week, we take a bus to Downtown Disney and walk to the Crossroads, and turn left to the Olive Garden where we can get a very good, inexpensive lunch prepaid. It breaks up the Disney crowd, and helps the pocketbook!
By PassPorter reader Susan B.

= money-saver   = time-saver   = magic-maker   = kid-friendly

Dining Tips (continued)

» Try Dessert at Kringla Bakeri

When one wants an enjoyable, light dessert, head over to the Kringla Bakeri in the Norway pavilion at Epcot. The "Veiled Maiden" is my all-time favorite, with its mixture of cream, apples, cinnamon, and bread crumbs. Perfect for a sunny afternoon. The bakery has other great treats but this one is just very refreshing yet takes care of the sweet tooth at the same time. Restaurant Akershus also has this as a larger portion on the menu.
By PassPorter reader Stefan

» Make Those Reservations

We just returned from a stay at Animal Kingdom Lodge and we couldn't believe that we couldn't get into any restaurants until 9:00 pm. Advance reservations are a must. My family laughed at me when I made a bunch before we left. I wish I would have made more. If you have a 3-year-old, you know 9:00 pm is a no go!
By PassPorter reader Amy

» Do a Character Meal Upon Arrival

When travelling with children, we always schedule a character dinner or lunch (depending on when you arrive) to sort of break the ice. Besides, my 5-year-old must see Mickey and Goofy before we do anything else.
By PassPorter reader Don L.

» Try 1900 Park Fare

If you are not staying at a resort on the monorail and plan on going to the Magic Kingdom in the morning, book a character breakfast early at 1900 Park Fare and use valet parking if you drive. When done with breakfast, hop on the monorail for a quick ride to the Magic Kingdom entrance. Be sure to ask to ride up front with the monorail driver, if possible! [Editor's Note: Disney's official policy on parking at the resorts is that parking for non-resort guests is "limited" and at certain times non-resort guests may not be permitted to park. Just something to keep in mind.]
By PassPorter reader Laura

» Bring Mickey Gloves to Character Meals

Buy a pair of Mickey gloves for your kids and take them to a character meal. The kids will get special attention from the characters, especially from Mickey, Minnie, and Donald. My child had a pair and will never forget the fun he had with the characters. Mickey and Minnie were giving him high-fives and Donald stole his gloves for while, but gave them back.
By PassPorter reader Stacey S.

Dining Tips (continued)

» *Try Chef Mickeys Your First Night*

We always stay at a Walt Disney World resort during our visits, but our arrivals are always later in the day so we don't want to use a day of our passes. Instead, we always get a reservation for an early evening dinner at Chef Mickey's at the Contemporary Resort. This character buffet has wonderful food and numerous characters that visit each and every table. This is just the thing to "get in the mood" for the days to come! If we have time afterward we catch the monorail to the Grand Floridian Resort and visit the shops and just take in the beautiful atmosphere. We're doing this again this July and we can't wait!
By PassPorter reader Jenice V.

» *Great Photos at Character Meals*

When eating at character meals, ask for a table next to the wall and seat your child(ren) there. When the characters come around for picture opportunities, you'll get a solid background for the photos—great shots with no other people in the background! (This is especially useful when you want to later enlarge a specific photo that came out great—without this, there's always someone in the background with a weird face that spoils the pictures!)
By PassPorter reader Lucia Z.

» *Getting Seats for Cinderella's*

When we were planning our daughter's first trip to Walt Disney World the only character she wanted to see was "Rella." Of course being the great planner that I am, and using my PassPorter as a guide, I knew that the character breakfast at Cinderella Castle sells out quickly. What I didn't realize was how quickly. 180 days out from our trip was a Saturday morning, but I got up at 6:45 am so that I could be on the phone by 7:00 am (that's when the reservations line opens). I got through at about 7:03 am and to my amazement, "Cindy's" was sold out. Well let me tell you I was angry (after all I got up early on a Saturday), frustrated (because my princess really wanted to meet Cinderella), and amazed that they could sell out that fast. I asked the cast member on the phone if there was anything she could suggest. Her suggestion (and my tip) was start calling back about two weeks before our arrival, be willing to take any time on any day during our stay, and to keep calling every day until we got a reservation. I started calling two weeks before our trip and on the second call I got a reservation for Cinderella's Royal Table for 7:50 am on a Monday morning. (Don't forget to ask for those early dining times on early entry mornings). [Editor's Note: I suggest you begin calling 407-WDW-DINE a few minutes before 7:00 am to allow time to navigate through the key prompts. I also suggest you state that "any available time" is acceptable when calling—this is more likely to yield success as the cast member doesn't have to fumble with days and times. Also have your credit card ready for your deposit.]
By PassPorter reader Janet M.

Dining Tips (continued)

» Breakfast is Best with Toddlers

When traveling to Disney with a toddler or infant, it's better to do character dining in the morning when kids are fresh and more apt for new experiences, not late in the day when they are tired and cranky. We have done three character meals in one trip and Donald's Dino breakfast in Disney's Animal Kingdom was by far the most enjoyable. Not to mention that Donald is one of the smallest characters there. My son (two at the time) really took to Donald the best.
By PassPorter reader Jodi B.

» Try Cinderella's Same Day

Every one always wants to have breakfast with Cinderella in the castle but the reservations book out several months in advance. We found that if you go in the morning directly to the castle and ask for a reservation for breakfast with Cinderella, they can sometimes accommodate you. If they can't, later in the day Cinderella sits in the restaurant's lobby and takes pictures with the kids (it is rare to see her anywhere else in the park).
By PassPorter reader Dunia

» Dine With Characters Early

Make your breakfast character meal reservations for as early as you can get your troop to the restaurant. I have found the restaurants to be less crowded, the "crowd" to be calmer (and better behaved), and the characters themselves to be more attentive earlier in the morning.
By PassPorter reader Ellen D.

» Do a Character Meal on Your Last Day

Since our last day didn't include parks (we drove), we decided to schedule a character breakfast for the morning of our departure. It turned out to be a great way to catch some last minute time with the characters and leave on a full stomach. We chose a nice, quiet breakfast at Cape May Cafe. We enjoyed it so much, that we are thinking of making it a tradition for our last mornings!
By PassPorter reader Maria

» Character Meals are a Must

If you are vacationing with small children, a character meal is a must. One our last trip to Disney, my daughter drove us crazy wanting to see Mickey Mouse as soon as possible, which we did. However, it was on about our third day there that we decided to have dinner at the Liberty Tree Tavern and it was the best thing we did. My daughter's eyes grew wide as Minnie, followed by other characters, came to our table. The look and smiles on her face as each character hugged her was priceless. We will be returning this fall and have quite a few character meals planned. They're the best.
By PassPorter reader Stephanie L.

= money-saver   = time-saver   = magic-maker   = kid-friendly

Dining Tips (continued)

» Get Down at the Hoop-Dee-Doo

If you have to choose from one "extra" thing, the Hoop-Dee-Doo Revue is a blast! It's corny but the kids love it and the food ain't too bad either.
By PassPorter reader Susan K.

» Combine Hoop Dee Do with Magic Kingdom

If you plan on attending Hoop De Doo one evening for dinner, try to make that a Magic Kingdom touring day. It is very easy and pleasant to take the boat from Magic Kingdom to Pioneer Hall. You can also return to Magic Kingdom on the boat making it a very pleasant evening all around!
By PassPorter reader Ruth Anne F.

» Book the Luau Early

If you're considering the Spirit of Aloha dinner show (luau) for small children, book early! It's a long show that will probably hold their interest only if they can see the stage well. The best seats go to the earliest bookings.
By PassPorter reader Mary B.

» Aloha Surprises

On this last trip to Walt Disney World resort we decided to do the Spirit of Aloha Dinner Show at the Polynesian. I found a stuffed Mickey and Minnie in Hawaiian-style attire on sale for $5.00 each at our local Disney Store. I purchased one pair and hid them in the suitcase. The day of the show when we all headed out to the bus stop I "remembered" that I had to "go potty" and quickly ducked into the room and pulled out the pair. I placed them on the bed. When we returned later on, our granddaughter was ecstatic to discover that Mickey and Minnie had visited and left her a gift. What fun! And she now has a huggable memory of that magical night and show!
By PassPorter reader Linda M.

© MediaMarx, Inc.

Making Magic Tips

» Listen to the Kids

After returning from an awesome trip to Walt Disney World with six children, our best piece of advice is to listen to the kids. Although we all enjoyed every part of our trip, the best memories are the ones the were not planned. Enjoying the family of ducks, watching a wedding at our hotel, and having a sandcastle contest were wonderful memories that we now have etched in our minds.
By PassPorter reader Jennifer P.

» Stop and Enjoy Your Surroundings

Just be open to the moment. Some of the best memories of our Walt Disney World vacation have been the "unexpected surprises." Be flexible enough in your plans to just stop and experience your surroundings. While advance dining reservations, touring schedules, and itineraries are all great tools to get you thinking about what you want to see and do on your trip, the best "plan" is to be spontaneous. By keeping this free-spirited attitude in mind, you will allow yourself to be enveloped in the Disney magic. Hear a great band playing in World Showcase but have an advance reservations in a few minutes? Why not stop for a listen instead? The line is long for Space Mountain and the FASTPASSes have long since run out. Just move on to another attraction like Carousel of Progress.
By PassPorter reader Michelle R.

» Try the Family Magic Tour

My daughter (8) and I did the Family Magic Tour at Magic Kingdom and, boy, did we have an excellent time. Our tour guide was so enthusiastic. We had to find Captain Hook's Hook or he would take over Magic Kingdom, and did we find it in the nick of time!! Even as an adult, I was caught up in the excitement. Definitely a must. And of course, it did cost extra. [Editor's Note: The tour is $27/person—the least expensive of all the Disney tours!]
By PassPorter reader Karen S.

= money-saver   = time-saver   = magic-maker   = kid-friendly

Making Magic Tips (continued)

» *Autographing Alternatives*

Instead of having your kids buy an autograph book, buy either a white Disney hat or T-shirt for the characters to sign. Our kids are more likely to be able to "show off" the autographs that they have received if they can wear them instead of showing them in a book. You also don't have to worry about pulling out the book every time that you see a character—they will likely have on the hat or the T-shirt. All you have to keep handy is the black marker. We have lost a number of autograph books, but our kids have a wonderful hat for each of our Disney trips. When we went on the cruise they each got two hats—one for the parks and one for the cruise. They proudly display them in their rooms and occasionally even wear them! They are also great conversation starters—we get comments on them everywhere that we go and it gives us a chance to talk "Disney" with others! [Editor's Note: If you want to have characters sign T-shirts, we recommend you do not wear it to the parks. Instead, carry it along with a hard surface (such as a stiff piece of cardboard) and present the T-shirt stretched over the hard surface for the character to sign.]
By PassPorter reader Cheryl M.

» *Visit Characters During the Parades*

Take your children to see characters during the parades. We found this extremely helpful with lines. We timed it just right during the afternoon parade and had a short wait.
By PassPorter reader Lori F.

» *Make Your Own Autograph Book*

If you have the time, make your own autograph book. Cut pictures out of magazines or the Disney one-a-day calendar. You can also find clip art online and print out the pictures. Then, glue the pictures into a spiral note card book or some other sturdy book. (I used a spiral princess notebook last time and scrapbook pages and a clipboard this time.) The characters are so great with the kids when they see their picture. Gov. Ratcliffe, Esmerelda, and Belle all sat with my sister for several minutes going through the book with her (and booing their nemesis).
By PassPorter reader Tia F.

» *Create a Disney Heirloom*

If you have young ones, get an autograph book as soon as you get there, and make sure you take a picture of your child/children with each character that signs the book. Once you get home and have your pictures developed, paste the corresponding picture opposite the autograph. It is an instant heirloom!
By PassPorter reader John C.

Making Magic Tips (continued)

» Finding Elusive Characters

Our son loves getting character autographs, and toward the end of each trip, he always has two or three characters that he is hunting down. When we are tracking down specific characters, we go to City Hall at Magic Kingdom after 9:00 am and they can find out where characters are throughout all the parks.
By PassPorter reader Diane M.

» Souvenir Pennies

In each of your children's packs, put in at least one roll of quarters and one roll of pennies. Why? For all the souvenir penny machines they'll want you to dig into your pockets for.
By PassPorter reader Dorie

» Pressed Penny Scavenger Hunt

Limiting the souvenirs was challenging, but we managed to keep the "buy-this" monster at bay. One of the things we did was to create a scavenger hunt for pressed pennies, even making up riddles for the particular penny and location. The girls were pleased with themselves as they determined where to look for the next penny to press. We provided a little plastic container with just enough quarters and pennies which they kept in their pouch. Our youngest liked the pressed pennies so much she made extras to take back to her friends!
By PassPorter reader Liz F.

» Use M&M Containers for Pressed Coins

Quarters and pennies for pressed pennies can be difficult to carry. Using the mini M&M tubes is a perfect solution. I carry one full of quarters, one full of pennies, and an extra one to put the pressed pennies in.
By PassPorter reader Tia F.

» Make Epcot Fun for Kids

To make the countries in Epcot more fun for the kids, play a treasure hunt game with them. Make up a fun list of simple things that they could find or do. When we went December, I had my son find out how to say "Merry Christmas" in each of the major countries. He had a great time doing it and showing off to all the relatives. This year I'll get him a camera and he'll have to take a picture of something funny in each country. And don't forget to have a special gift for the kids once they complete their assignment!
By PassPorter reader Becky M.

Making Magic Tips (continued)

» Do An Amazing Race

On our fourth trip to Disney we were looking for something fun to plan for the kids to do. I created an Amazing Race game, Disney style. The kids (ages 11 and 13) teamed up against my sister and I to compete at various tasks. For example, we had to find the name of restaurants, get autographs, eat ice cream, find cast members with certain names, etc. We had the best time doing this. We kept the game central to only monorail locations but it was a blast for us all. I am really not sure who had more fun—us or the kids.
By PassPorter reader Wendy B.

» Fuji Waterproof Cameras

I always take a bunch of Fuji waterproof cameras. They are at least $5 less than Kodak waterproof cameras—I buy them at Wal-mart. We spend a lot of time at the water parks and have a ball taking photos of ourselves in the water.
By PassPorter reader Stephanie L.

» Preserve Your Kids' Memories

During our last trip, I had my children write down their thoughts at the end of each day. I sealed these in individual envelopes and put them in the appropriate PassPorter pocket. This allowed me to use all of the space on the PassPorter pocket for my thoughts of the day and still have my sons' priceless thoughts kept safely along with mine. We plan to open the envelopes and read them the night before we leave for our next trip in October. I am sure this will build the excitement for all of us! Their entries will then be resealed and put back in the PassPorter, which goes into the Disney memory box we have started. I cant wait for my PassPorter to be filled with memories!
By PassPorter reader Kristi

» Turn Your PassPorter into a Scrapbook

"Scrapbook" your PassPorter!! I had this idea while I was printing out an image of me for inside the front cover of my PassPorter. If you have digital images from your vacation, print them off on adhesive backed sheets (1.5" labels work well). Then cut them apart. You can add the sticker pictures from your trip around the text area in the PassPorter! That way not only do you have your photo memories, but when you show your friends the photos they can read about where you were in the book! Scrapbook stores have lots of different stickers and labels that you can use to decorate the PassPorter into an awesome memory album!! Use a highlighter throughout the book and write in your own notes on the blank labels, get creative!
By PassPorter reader Kristen V.

Making Magic Tips (continued)

» Through A Child's Eye

Before our last Disney trip, we gave our two oldest daughters their own cameras and film to take on vacation. They took some wonderful pictures, and it was through those pictures that we saw things through a child's eyes. As adults, sometimes we miss the really important things to kids. They both have nice photo albums with their "memories" in them. You could also help your child make up a scrapbook with their wonderful photos and souvenirs.
By PassPorter reader Marjie G.

» Chart Your Kids Growth at Disney

To create a Disney growth chart, take a picture of your child standing next to the same thing on every vacation. Every year we take a photo of each child next to the Native American statue in Magic Kingdom, plus a group picture. This makes a great collage! [Editor's Note: I'm fond of the you-must-be-this-tall-to-ride signs myself. Pick your favorite!]
By PassPorter reader Donna F.

» Ask Others to Photograph You

Speak up and get those photo opportunities! After numerous vacations with my husband, I realized we did not have many photos of us together. Since we typically travel by ourselves, all of our photos were of each of us separately. Now to solve this, we have learned to speak up. We ask nearby park guests or cast members to snap our photo together. This way we have "separate" photos and "couple photos." This would also be a good idea for families, groups, etc. so everyone can be in the photo together.
By PassPorter reader Michelle R.

» Mark Canisters to Avoid Double Exposing

I take a lot of photos when I am at Walt Disney World and I have come up with a way to keep my "taken" rolls of film separate from my "untaken" rolls. I pack some of my self adhesive address labels in my camera case and when I am finished with a roll of film I attach one of them to the film canister to identify it as a "taken" roll. In the past I have been known to double expose rolls and to have processed empty rolls of film! This doesn't happen anymore!
By PassPorter reader Sue N.

» Take a Photo in Mickey's Ears

We like to go to the Contemporary and take a family photo in the huge Mickey ears behind the resort. We then send out the photo to share with family and friends for Christmas cards. It's easy to do since they have a stand that holds your camera and you can take the picture by yourself using the remote button (or timer) on the camera! It's a wonderful way to have your Disney memories shared and remembered all year long!
By PassPorter reader Stephanie N.

= money-saver   = time-saver   = magic-maker   = kid-friendly

Making Magic Tips (continued)

» ABC, These Pictures You Have to See!

Ok, I am a scrapbook nut. I make sure that every single event in our lives is recorded. Naturally, our first trip to Walt Disney World is no exception. So, before we even went to Disney, I put together (with help from suggestions on the message boards) the ABCs of Disney. That way, while we're there, I'll know what pictures I really want to get. The ABC's go like this: A is for Arrival a vacation dream come true, B is for Breakfast with Mickey and Minnie too! C is for Caribbean Beach where we rest our weary heads, D is for Dale and Chip a couple of furry friends, E is for Epcot with its famous silver ball, F is for Food plenty of snacks for us all, G is for Gepetto and his little wooden boy, H is for happiness faces painted with joy, I is for ice cream chocolate Mickey bars, J is for Jasmine Aladdin's princess from afar, K is for Kingdom where the magic all begins, L is for Lion King and all his rowdy friends, M is for Mickey one special mouse is he, N is for nightfall and the marvelous sights to see, O is for Out of the Ordinary the magic that unfolds, P is for Parade a spectacle to behold, Q is for quiet time a much needed rest, R is for resort only the very best, S is for Small World where children sing together, T is for Tiki Room and its many birds of feather, U is for Unexpected surprise at the end of each day, V is for Villains and keeping them at bay, W is for Wonderland and a little girl named Alice, X is for "Xtra" special a birthday at the Crystal Palace, Y is for Young at heart the Disney in us all, Z is for Zippity-Doo-Dah we really had a ball! I don't have the pictures yet, but I know our scrapbook is going to turn out cute as can be and our memories will last forever!
By PassPorter reader Darcie G.

» Create a Disney Scrapbook

I create a large scrapbook of our Disney memories after each trip (photos, memorabilia, journaling of memories, and so on). My husband always brings a laptop along with us. When we get back to our room in the evenings, it's nice to have each family member tell what their favorite parts of the day were while they're still fresh on the mind. I type everything in as we talk about it. Then when I get home, get the pictures developed, and start to work on the scrapbook, all those precious memories have already been preserved and are just waiting on me to use them in the scrapbook!
By PassPorter reader Amy S.

» Create a Virtual Keepsake Memory

While this tip takes a bit of web site design ability, it makes for an outstanding keepsake to share with family members. Use your PassPorter to keep a diary of each day's events, i.e. how you got to the park, your sequence of rides throughout the day, special comments or funny quotes by folks in your party. Capture it all as a daily diary by creating web pages after you return, linking all your images from your trip to each day's diary. Link in a bit of Disney music and burn it all to a CD. Share this special keepsake with family and friends!
By PassPorter reader Alan L.

Making Magic Tips (continued)

» Bright Clothing Makes For Good Photos

When catching your magical memories on film, try to wear brightly-colored clothing. We find that the best photos are the ones where our children are dressed in bright clothes. And these tend to be their favorite photos to look at over and over again to relive those special magical moments.
By PassPorter reader Deanna S.

» Don't Flash Through Glass

One of the biggest things that frustrates me is seeing people taking pictures "through" glass with a flash. If you're trying to take a picture of the fish, etc. at The Seas you're probably only going to end up with a great shot of the flash reflecting back at you! Also, shooting out a window with a flash will often have the same disastrous results. For the best photos, turn that flash off when you've got glass nearby.
By PassPorter reader Mark F.

» Offer to Photograph Others

You can really be a big help to people you see taking pictures by offering to "help out." One person—whether it's a group of two or two-hundred—gets left out of the picture. You have to decide quickly if they seem like having a stranger approach them and offering to take the picture for them is something they won't be nervous about. I've never had someone turn me down. It just takes a little common sense in your approach. I've even done it for people who speak a different language. A little imagination with sign language gets the point across.
By PassPorter reader Mark F.

» Identify and Track Your Vacation Photos

My husband loves to take pictures, but we like to keep them in order of our trip. Last time we worked together as a team and he unloaded/loaded the camera while I dug out the film and stored it back away in his camera bag. What helped us a lot was that I stuck a red Sharpie marker in the bag. As each roll of film was finished I simply numbered that roll and stored it back in the canister. Each night we kept track of which rolls had been taken in our PassPorter so we could start out on the correct number the next morning. When we got home and went to develop the film we simply wrote the number from the film onto the film developing package. It helped us to know which ones were ready, but it also kept the developer from losing any of our pictures. This really came in handy since we had 19 rolls of film!
By PassPorter reader Lisa

Making Magic Tips (continued)

» Make a Photo Timeline at Disney

If you are a repeat traveler to Walt Disney World, pick a favorite spot to take your family's picture at each year. This way, over the years you will get a timeline of your family's trips. Once you have enough photos like these, you can even put them into their own frame or scrapbook, where you can see how you (and the spot you picked) changed from year to year. These make great gifts, especially for your kids to show them their childhood at Walt Disney World. We always take our picture with our Walk Around The World brick. We have pictures with it each year from 1995 to the present. It's fun to look back (and laugh!) at the old ones.
By PassPorter reader Jacquelyn H.

» Keep Track of Photo Days

While honeymooning in Walt Disney World, my daughter Diana and her new husband Scott would stand in front of the bus designation sign of the park they were heading to that day. If it were day one, and they were going to Magic Kingdom, Diana would have her picture snapped in front of the Magic Kingdom bus sign, holding up one finger; on day two, if they went to Animal Kingdom, she stood in front of the Animal Kingdom bus sign with two fingers up, etc. This way they had a pictorial record of what park they went to on what day!
By PassPorter reader Debbie H.

» Write a Journal

We relive our Disney vacations over and over again by creating trip journals. We give each of our four children a journal in which to write a story at the end of each day. We tell the kids that their journals will be graded: $10 for an "A," $7.50 for a "B," and so on. They haven't figured out that they always get an "A" because they're priceless to us. And it's fun months later to get the journals out and re-live the adventure.
By PassPorter reader Joy C.

» Edible Souvenirs

A wonderful, edible souvenir for those who didn't get to go to Disney with you is the rice crispie mouse bars that can be bought at most resort restaurants.
By PassPorter reader Anonymous

» Visit Belz Outlet Mall

Buy your souvenirs and gifts at the Disney Outlet at Belz before going to the parks. It is much cheaper, you will not have to carry them around the parks, it will save you time otherwise used in shopping at the parks, and it will ease your mind.
By PassPorter reader Stephen G.

= money-saver   = time-saver   = magic-maker   = kid-friendly

Making Magic Tips (continued)

» Buy Souvenirs Before You Go

I like to buy a lot of souvenirs before we leave for people that aren't going to be on the trip. I go to the local Disney Store and shop the Disney Catalog to buy gifts for Mom, Dad, brothers, sisters etc. and get them before we leave. That way we have more room for our souvenirs and less stuff to bring home. No one knows the difference, plus a lot of the times the stuff is cheaper than at Walt Disney World.
By PassPorter reader Trish S.

» Cheap Souvenirs

Do you want to bring back something for your kid's classmates? Or for you coworkers? Souvenirs can get pretty expensive. Well, you can pick a bunch of small gifts the next time you wait in line at one of the resort's fast food service counters! That's right—most fast food service counters at the Disney-owned resorts (and in some of the parks) sell "Mickey Mouse-shaped icon" straws for about 50 cents. They come in a variety of colors: clear, red, blue, green, and yellow. They're inexpensive, easy to carry, and only found in Disney! Now you can buy for all of your kid's classmates and have some cash left over for your own souvenirs. Happy Shopping!
By PassPorter reader Kurt G.

» Great Gift Idea on a Budget

If you want to take gifts home for family and friends and have a small budget, go to the Main Street Confectionery in the Magic Kingdom and buy bags of sweets for everyone. Then at any other Disney merchandise store (inside the park or in your resort), buy a package of Disney character pens (big beautiful pens with Disney characters on them). Open the package and attach one pen to each bag of sweets you purchased with a ribbon! These make great inexpensive gifts and your friends and family are sure to love them!
By PassPorter reader Lucia Z.

» Making Priceless Memories

I went to Walt Disney World when I was 8 years old and I got a Minnie Mouse hat. I still have it and love it! A little extra money spend on something cute is priceless compared to the memories I have and remember about that magical week at Walt Disney World.
By PassPorter reader Leah G.

= money-saver   = time-saver   = magic-maker   = kid-friendly

Making Magic Tips (continued)

» Replace Ripped Ponchos

On a recent trip I had to purchase five rain ponchos. I quickly discovered the real value of these ponchos when my son ripped his the first day! A cast member heard me talking to my son about how he ripped it and she quickly told me that all rain ponchos purchased in Walt Disney World are replaced free of charge if they tear or rip! It's not only at the shop where you purchased them either. My husband ripped his on the last day and a gift store inside Magic Kingdom replaced his just as easily. *By PassPorter reader Colleen A.*

» Photo Albums Make Good Souvenirs

Buy a photo album as a souvenir! They come in all price ranges and sizes. Some have the year on them and they have new "themes" each year. It will be a great reminder and organize all those magical pictures into one great Disney memory. *By PassPorter reader Kim L.*

» Send Audio Postcards Home

Sure, regular postcards are fun... but audio postcards are even better, and faster, too! Just take your cell phone with you to Walt Disney World and call your family and friends from inside a relatively noisy attraction. For example, phone your Aunt Jeanne while riding "it's a small world," put on speakerphone, and she can hear the wonderful notes of that unforgettable song! Just before you hang-up, you can quietly leave a message so as not to disturb other guests around you. For example, "Having a great time—guess where we are!" I'd only suggest this for attractions that aren't so quiet that a cell phone would bother others. *By PassPorter reader Lynn*

» Get Name Badges

Buy Disney name badges for the kids in one of the parks. They look similar to the badges worn by cast members, but can be personalized for your kids. The cast members notice the badges and will often call your children by their names. The kids really get a kick out of this. *By PassPorter reader Diane K.*

» Pin Trading is Good for Kids

Our six-year-old granddaughter really got into Disney pin trading last year. As she collected and traded pins, she wanted to keep some of them. To avoid confusion and to save time when trading, we got a second lanyard and attached her "keepables" to that one. She wanted me to wear the lanyard that held her treasures. Then, whenever she approached a cast member to look at pins and negotiate, she always had me in tow. She introduced me each time to whomever she was speaking. She appeared more confident to walk up to a stranger with me holding her hand. Pin trading is a great social skill and confidence builder for children (and adults). Needless to say, we have a wonderful pin collection! *By PassPorter reader Elizabeth W.*

= money-saver   = time-saver   = magic-maker   = kid-friendly

Making Magic Tips (continued)

» Order a Gift Basket

To make things extra special for our daughter, we ordered a gift basket from Disney that included an autograph book and pen, a Disney beanie, and several other items. We ordered it so it will be there when we arrive at the hotel. We also didn't sign our names but signed it "Hope you'll have a great time" and she may think that Mickey sent it to her, which would be very special! Also with getting the autograph book and pen, she will be all ready to get some character signatures. [Editor's Note: You can order gift baskets at 1-407-827-3505.]
By PassPorter reader Cindy

» Evening Monorail Rides

We usually stay at a monorail resort. When our kids were small they'd often fall asleep on a late evening car ride so we'd help them unwind on vacation by taking a late evening ride on the monorail from our resort. It helped them calm down and most nights we'd get on with two excited kids and get off with kids who were now asleep in our arms. Even as teens now they still like to take one last loop around the line before calling it a night.
By PassPorter reader Stephanie L.

» Food and Fireworks Fun

Make the most of that evening meal by planning it around a fireworks show! You can watch the Magic Kingdoms fireworks from the California Grill high atop the Contemporary, sit outside on the verandah of Narcoosees at the Grand Floridian, or watch from the Polynesian's Ohana. The lights are dimmed and the music accompanies the show—it makes a very memorable meal! At Epcot great viewing for IllumiNations can be found from the patio of the Rose and Crown at United Kingdom and the Cantina de San Angel at Mexico, too. Don't be afraid to tell your server that's why you're there—they may help you get the best seating and let you linger until the show's over! Some of my most favorite Walt Disney World memories are of sharing food and fireworks with those who are special to me.
By PassPorter reader Carole W.

© MediaMarx, Inc.

Making Magic Tips (continued)

» Two Firework Shows in One Evening

Have dinner at the California Grill on top of Contemporary and schedule it during the fireworks over Magic Kingdom! There is a wonderful balcony off of the restaurant where you have the "bird's eye" view of the fireworks. They even pipe in the music soundtrack! I recommend you make your advance reservation for about 45-60 minutes before fireworks time depending on the season and how crowded you expect it to be to try and time the fireworks just before dessert. Tell your server what you are up to and they will usually accommodate. If you really get it right order your dessert/coffee/etc. before the show for delivery right after. When it gets close to the scheduled time leave your table and go outside for the show returning to your table for a delightful finish to your meal! If fireworks timing allows, based on season, you may be able to see two fireworks shows. There is a wonderful little room in restaurant corner furthest from Magic Kingdom where you can also see Epcot IllumiNations fireworks in the distance (no soundtrack). As that show is longer than Magic Kingdom, we were once able to savor our post fireworks dessert while watching the Epcot fireworks in the distance from a window side table. Also this room is much quieter and intimate than the main restaurant area.
By PassPorter reader Michael S.

» Give Pixie Gifts

Buy a Disney character or a few items on sale at the Disney Store (or your local discount store). Bring these with you to Walt Disney World as a "pixie gift." Surprise your children each morning with these "pixie gifts." This will reduce the gimmies and your children will have a surprise in the morning (and it will save some $$'s in your wallet!).
By PassPorter reader Wendy

» Fireworks in a Ferry Boat

We came across this tip by complete accident. We were camping at Fort Wilderness and headed down to the beach at Bay Lake to watch the fireworks. As we were standing on the beach, we started to talk to the captain of the ferry that crosses Bay Lake into the Magic Kingdom. He asked if we were waiting for the fireworks and we said, "Yes." He told us to hop onboard and we'd have a beautiful view of them as we crossed the lake. We got on the boat and saw the most spectacular site. We almost seemed to be going into the fireworks and the peace on the water really intensified the effect. You really must do this!! [Editor's Note: Timing your boat ride to coincide with the fireworks can be tricky, but it is a delightful experience. It works with the ferry boats that leave from Grand Floridian, Polynesian, and Contemporary, too.]
By PassPorter reader Colleen A.

= money-saver   = time-saver   = magic-maker   = kid-friendly

Making Magic Tips (continued)

» Pick a Day for Relaxation

One of our most memorable days at Disney World was a day that we didn't have any plans. We had been going full tilt for three days trying to cram as much as we could in our short stay and everyone was getting really grouchy. We decided to toss the schedule for the day and hopped on the first bus without seeing where it was going and spent the morning at that park. In the afternoon, we went back and relaxed at the hotel. We made reservations at Marrakesh and had a relaxing dinner and an early night. The next day, we were rested and ready to once again follow our scheduled must-see attractions.
By PassPorter reader Heather

» Celebrate with a Fireworks Cruise

I like to make reservations for the "moonlight cruise" to see the fireworks—it's great for a birthday or anniversary. As this cruise can be quite expensive, I would suggest bringing your own snacks and champagne. You can even bring your own balloons! My husband and I did this to celebrate our 20th anniversary last June after a wonderful dinner at Ohana and a stroll along the Polynesian beach to see the Electrical Water Pageant on the Seven Seas Lagoon. We can't wait to do it again!
By PassPorter reader Margaret W.

» Dress Your Girls in Princess Shirts

If your daughter is into the Disney Princesses (mine adores them!) dress her in a shirt that says Princess on it. My 4-year-old could not read her shirt, so she was so surprised when cast members would said "Good Morning, Princess" or "Watch your step, Princess!" She said to me "Mommy, guess what? They think I am a real Princess here!" It was really precious and she got lots of attention all day!
By PassPorter reader Christy H.

» Capture Your Family and the Parade

If your family is enjoying the parade, cross the street to photograph them. You can get some really neat shots of the parade and your family's reactions to the fun.
By PassPorter reader Barbara G.

» Name the Celebrities

Here's a fun game to make the time pass while on line or on the way home. How many attractions can you name that have celebrity guest(s) starring in them? (i.e. Ellen Degeneres in Universe of Energy). Make the game harder by seeing how many celebrity voices you can come up with!
By PassPorter reader Beth S.

Making Magic Tips (continued)

» Get Certificates for "Big" Rides

If you are enjoying Walt Disney World with young children, stop at the attractions they cannot yet ride (due to height restrictions) and ask if there is a special non-rider certificate. There may be one signed by a Disney character that they can have. They'll love it!
By PassPorter reader Myra P.

» Gregarious is Good

Disney cast members look for animated and enthusiastic couples/families to be the Grand Marshals in their parades. Ask questions and talk to park employees, especially around the tip boards. You never know who is looking for the next Grand Marshal!
By PassPorter reader Kim M.

» Personalize Your Shirts

I used Avery Dark T-shirt Transfers to make personalized shirts for all five members of our family. I found inexpensive Hanes T-shirts in a different color for each day and used Disney's Magic Artist software or clipart from Disney web sites to create a different design for each set of shirts. I also added some personalization to the designs, like "Powell Family Vacation" or "Powell Family 2009" to the designs. The shirts worked great for helping to keep track of my husband and three boys. We also got extra attention from cast members who would say things like "Have a great day, Mr. Powell!", etc. At least ten different people chased us down to ask where we got our shirts. The shirts looked almost professional and only cost around $6 each.
By PassPorter reader Kris P.

» Tour the World on the Monorail

Take some time to ride the monorail, even if you don't need it for transportation. The route from the Ticket & Transportation Center to Epcot is long, scenic, and relaxing! And as a bonus, the monorail does a circuit over Future World, giving you a unique perspective of the park!
By PassPorter reader Erin

» Leave Little Gifts to Be Discovered

A couple of years back I purchased two complete collections of Disney Pins that depicted a different Disney Character on each of the fifty United States. These pins will travel (hidden better than many Hidden Mickeys) to Disney with us on our upcoming trip. Each day as we leave our room, I will slip back to check on something/anything and we will set out several pins for our grandchildren to discover upon returning at the end of the day. We did something similar on our last trip and the kids thought Mickey brought them gifts while we were out.
By PassPorter reader Redonna L.

Making Magic Tips (continued)

» Get Your Do at the Barber Shop

Don't miss the barber shop in Main Street's town square at the Magic Kingdom. My sons have been getting their hair cut there, along with their Daddy, since they were 1. The Mickey-shaped sprinkles and colored hair gel are always a highlight of the trip for my boys. Also they have a blast with all the attention they get. [Editor's Note: I totally agree—this is fantastic experience. My son's only haircuts have been at the Harmony Barber Shop. They even give a "first haircut" certificate to little ones. Love it!]
By PassPorter reader Rhonda M.

» Glowing Hair

There is a hair gel called "göt2b shocking" firm-hold sculpting gel. It looks and acts like regular hair gel, but it glows under dark lights. My boys used it on the days we did dark rides. They had a hoot looking at each other, heads a-glow! My older son even sat through the "baby rides" happily with this as a diversion! [Editor's Visit http://www.got2b.com for an online coupon.]
By PassPorter reader Beth W.

» Take a Birthday Cruise!

Disney birthday parties are great and reasonably priced! On our last trip we took a pontoon boat ride from the BoardWalk to the middle of the "pond" at Epcot for a close up view of IllumiNations, then cruised around some of the waterways. For about $275 you get a cake with a choice of Disney characters made out of white chocolate, soft drinks, chips, munchies, and party hats. And you can take up to 10 people on the boat. The photos we were able to get made it worth the money-everything else was a bonus! [Editor's Note: Prices will depend on what you want, of course. I've had several parties on pontoon boats at Disney and they were all a blast! For more information, call 407-WDW-PLAY.]
By PassPorter reader Anne S.

» Celebrate a Birthday

Plan a trip when one member of your party celebrates a birthday, and make sure to tell the cast members you meet about the special occasion. They will make the birthday a very magical day. You can also get a "Today is my Birthday" pin at Guest Services in all four theme parks.
By PassPorter reader Mirjam

= money-saver   = time-saver   = magic-maker   = kid-friendly

Making Magic Tips (continued)

» Share Your Celebration

Let everyone know if you are celebrating anything (ex. birthday, anniversary, or other). I received a free desert at one restaurant, champagne at a lounge in my hotel, and then a nice chocolate gift left in my room. The second time I went I wore a T-shirt announcing my anniversary trip and received even more surprises. Don't be shy—celebrate with Disney and they may celebrate with you.
By PassPorter reader Penny R.

» Ears to the Honeymoon

If you are going to WDW for your honeymoon, purchase the honeymoon ears upon arrival. The groom's ears are a black top hat with Mickey ears, and the bride's ears are a white cap with Minnie ears and a wedding veil. On our honeymoon, we wore these ears everywhere we went in the "World." We were greeted by almost every cast member with a "Congratulations!" or received special attention. Little extras like these really added to our experience!
By PassPorter reader Mario A.

» Tinker Bell Kisses for Birthdays

In advance of our trip (which celebrated our granddaughter's fifth birthday), I purchased a package of star-shaped "glitter" that is used for party tables (each star is only about 1/8th" in size). I also went to our local Disney Store and purchased several small fun but inexpensive sale items. I hid them in my suitcase. Each night after Kaitlin fell asleep I would sneak one item and a few stars out and put them next to the phone. As soon as Mickey woke us, I placed the object on her pillow and sprinkled her hair and pillow with stars, and placed one on her cheek. She was always so excited to see what gift Tinker Bell left on her pillow along with her morning Tinker Bell wake-up kisses! She saved every star carefully to bring home to show mommy and daddy.
By PassPorter reader Linda M.

» Give "Rein(deer)" Checks

While at Walt Disney World this year we came across several items that were a must on our nephew's Christmas list. We knew we did not have time for Santa to bring them, so we issued each child a "Rein(deer)" check for the item saying it was very popular and Santa did not have enough to go around but they would receive it as soon as possible. Kind of a cute idea to give more time to come up with that hard-to-get gift!
By PassPorter reader Gennie B.

SAVE! = money-saver   **Speedy** = time-saver   **Magic** = magic-maker   **Kids** = kid-friendly

30% Discount Coupon

Save 30% off _any_ PassPorter guidebook (_see below for title list_) when you order direct from the publisher!

How to order a PassPorter at your 30% discount:
1. Visit http://www.passporterstore.com/store to view our guidebooks and place an order (type in this discount code during checkout: friend).
2. Call us toll-free at 877-WAYFARER (that's 1-877-929-3273) and mention the "disney500" code when placing your order.

This offer valid only for direct book sales through PassPorter Travel Press, an imprint of MediaMarx, Inc. Offer not valid in bookstores. Cannot be combined with other discounts. Discount code: disney500

Popular PassPorter Print Titles

All of the following titles are eligible for your 30% discount!

PassPorter's Walt Disney World—The unique travel guide, planner, organizer, journal, and keepsake! (spiral, deluxe starter kit, and refill kit)

PassPorter's Speed Planner—A fast, easy method for planning practically perfect vacations, great for busy people! (paperback)

PassPorter's Disney Vacation Club—Tips for members and members-to-be, filled with practial information! (paperback)

PassPorter's Open Mouse for Walt Disney World—Easy-Access Trips for Travelers With Extra Challenges. Covers virtually every special challenge! (paperback)

PassPorter's Disney Cruise Line and Its Ports of Call—The take-along travel guide and planner. The most comprehensive guide to Disney cruising! (paperback)

PassPorter's Disney Cruise Clues—A tried-and-true collection of more than 250 tips for Disney Cruise Line vacations. (paperback)

PassPorter's Disneyland Resort and Southern California Attractions—The unique travel guide, planner, organizer, journal, and keepsake! (spiral, deluxe starter kit, and refill kit)

PassPorter's Treasure Hunts at Walt Disney World—Discover what everyone else is missing with more than 100+ hunts for a variety of ages and skills (paperback)

More information about PassPorter's innovative guidebooks and descriptions of each of the above titles are on the following pages.

PassPorter's Club

Do you want more help planning your Disney vacation? Join the PassPorter's Club and get all these benefits:

✔ "All-you-can-read" access to EVERY e-book we publish (12 titles at press time). PassPorter's Club passholders also get early access to these e-books before the general public. New e-books are added on a regular basis, too.

✔ Interactive, customizable "e-worksheets" to help make your trip planning easier, faster, and smoother. These are the electronic, interactive worksheets we've been mentioning throughout this book. The worksheets are in PDF format and can be printed for a truly personalized approach! We have more than 50 worksheets, with more on the way. You can see a sample e-worksheet to the right.

✔ Access to super-sized "e-photos" in the PassPorter Photo Archives—photos can be zoomed in up to 25 times larger than standard web photos. You can use these e-photos to see detail as if you're actually standing there—or use them for desktop wallpaper, scrapbooking, whatever!

✔ Our best discount on print guidebooks ... 35% off!

There's more features, too! For a full list of features and current e-books, e-worksheets, and e-photos, visit http://www.passporter.com/club. You can also take a peek inside the Club's Gallery at http://www.passporterboards.com/forums/passporters-club-gallery. The Gallery is open to everyone—it contains two FREE interactive e-worksheets to try out!

Price: A PassPorter's Club pass is currently $4.95/month, or the cost of just one e-book!

How to Get Your Pass to the PassPorter's Club

Step 1. Get a free community account. Register simply and quickly at http://www.passporterboards.com/forums/register.php.

Step 2. Log in at http://www.passporterboards.com/forums/login.php using the Member Name and password you created in step 1.

Step 3. Get your pass. Select the type of pass you'd like and follow the directions to activate it immediately. We currently offer monthly and annual passes. (Annual passes save 25% and get extra perks!)

Questions? Assistance? We're here to help! Please send e-mail to club@passporter.com.

You may also find many of your questions answered in our FAQ (Frequently Asked Questions) in the Gallery forum (see link above).

What is PassPorter?

PassPorters are unique, all-in-one travel guides that offer comprehensive, expert advice and innovative planning systems. Many of our guidebooks feature built-in worksheets and organizer "PassPockets." The PassPockets help you organize your vacation by building trip itineraries on the front before you go, storing maps, passes, and receipts inside while you're there, recording memories and expenses on the back to enjoy when you return.

PassPorter Walt Disney World Resort

It all started with Walt Disney World (and a mouse)! Our general Walt Disney World guidebook covers everything you need to plan a practically perfect vacation, including fold-out park maps; full-color photos and charts; resort room layout diagrams; KidTips; descriptions, reviews, and ratings for the resorts, parks, attractions, and restaurants; and much more!

This edition also includes 14 organizer pockets you can use to plan your trip before you go, hold papers while you're there, and record your memories for when you return. The PassPockets are our readers' #1 favorite feature because they make planning, organizing, and capturing your vacation very easy.

Learn more and order at http://www.passporter.com, or get a copy at your favorite bookstore. Our Walt Disney World guide is available in a spiral-bound edition, and a Deluxe Edition in a ring binder with interior pockets is also available—see the next page. Don't take our word for it—ask others what they think of PassPorter. Here's a letter we recently received (printed with permission).

Listen, I'm not well organized. OK, that's an understatement. I'm a mess. I don't plan either. I'm more fly by the seat of my pants. However, 6 years ago on my honeymoon, my husband and I wandered aimlessly around Disney World and didn't get to see half the stuff we wanted and didn't even know about the other half.

So, my first trip with my daughter would have to be different. I found the boards at http://www.disboards.com and asked what book I needed to buy. Most everyone suggested yours. "What would I do with pockets?" I asked myself.

Through the planning stages, I found myself furiously writing different phone numbers, confirmation numbers, and other important information into my Passporter. I stuffed all kinds of information and plans into those pockets.

When we got to Disney, my husband could not believe how organized I was. Check-ins were a breeze. I had all the information I needed at my fingertips. I think his mouth was hanging open at one point. He'd say, "What's on the agenda for today?" And I'd whip out my book and tell him.

I had touring plans so we knew exactly where to go when. The lady at the Rainforest Café could not believe I had all my info right there for her. I think she thought I am always that organized. (Can you make a Passporter for my regular life?)

My vacation could not have gone any smoother and I owe it all to you!

Thanks so much,

Sydonie Davis

More PassPorters

You've asked for more PassPorters—we've listened! We have four PassPorter print books and ten e-books (and growing), all designed to make your Disney vacation the best it can be. And if you've wished for a PassPorter with all the flexibility and features of a daily planner, check out our Deluxe Editions (described below). To learn more about the new PassPorters and get release dates, please visit us at http://www.passporter.com.

PassPorter's Walt Disney World Deluxe Edition

Design first-class vacations with this loose-leaf ring binder edition. The Deluxe Edition features the same great content as *PassPorter's Walt Disney World* spiral guide. Special features of the Deluxe Edition include ten interior storage slots in the binder to hold guidemaps, ID cards, and a pen (we even include a pen). The Deluxe PassPorter binder makes it really easy to add, remove, and rearrange pages ... you can even download, print, and add in updates, feature articles, and supplemental pages from our web site, and refills are available for purchase. Learn more at http://www.passporter.com/wdw/deluxe. htm. The Deluxe Edition is available through bookstores by special order—the ISBN is 978-1-58771-083-4 (2011 Deluxe Edition), or search for the latest edition.

PassPorter's Disney Cruise Line and its Ports of Call

Updated annually! Get your cruise plans in shipshape with our updated, award-winning field guide ... includes details on all new ports and the new ships to come!

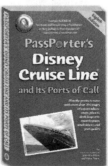

Authors Jennifer and Dave Marx cover the Disney Cruise Line in incredible detail, including deck plans, stateroom floor plans, original photos, menus, entertainment guides, port/shore excursion details, and plenty of worksheets to help you budget, plan, and record your information. We also include reader tips, photos, and magial memories! In its ninth edition in 2011, this is the original and most comprehensive guidebook devoted to the Disney Cruise Line! Learn more and order your copy at http://www.passporter.com/dcl or get a copy at your favorite bookstore. ISBN for the eighth edition paperback, no PassPockets is 978-1-58771-079-7. Also available in a Deluxe Edition with organizer PassPockets (ISBN: 978-1-58771-080-3).

Even More PassPorters

PassPorter's Disneyland Resort and Southern California Attractions— Second Edition

PassPorter tours the park that started it all in this updated book! California's Disneyland, Disney's California Adventure, and Downtown Disney get PassPorter's expert treatment, and we throw in Hollywood and Downtown Los Angeles, San Diego, SeaWorld, the San Diego Zoo and Wild Animal Park, LEGOLAND, and Six Flags Magic Mountain. All this, and PassPorter's famous PassPockets and planning features. Our second edition follows the same format as the 2010 edition of PassPorter's Walt Disney World, complete with glossy, full-color pages, tons of photos from your authors and fellow readers, and plenty of brand-new pages! We een include the special photo supplement at the end to get you in the mood for our California  vacation. Whether you're making the pilgrimage to Disneyland for a big celebration or planning a classic Southern California family vacation, you can't miss. Learn more at http://www.passporter.com/dl, or pick it up at your favorite bookstore (ISBN: 978-1-58771-042-1). This guidebook is also available as a Deluxe Edition in a padded, six-ring binder (ISBN: 978-1-58771-043-8).

PassPorter's Treasure Hunts at Walt Disney World

Have even more fun at Walt Disney World! Jennifer and Dave's treasure hunts have long been a favorite part of PassPorter reader gatherings at Walt Disney World, and now you can join in the fun. Gain a whole new appreciation of Disney's fabulous attention to detail as you search through the parks and resorts for the little (and big) things that you may never have noticed before. Great for individuals, families, and groups, with hunts for people of all ages and levels of Disney knowledge. Special, "secure" answer pages make sure nobody can cheat. Learn more, see sample hunts, and order your copy at http://www.passporter.com/hunts or get a copy at your favorite bookstore (ISBN: 978-1-58771-026-1).

PassPorter E-Books

We have many e-books that cover narrower topics in delightful depth! See all the details at http://www.passporterstore.com/store/ebooks.aspx. And watch for select e-books to make it into print in the near future.

Register Your PassPorter

We are <u>very</u> interested to learn how your vacation went and what you think of the PassPorter, how it worked (or didn't work) for you, and your opinion on how we could improve it! We encourage you to register your copy of PassPorter with us—in return for your feedback, we'll send you **two valuable coupons** good for discounts on PassPorters and PassHolder pouches when purchased directly from us. You can register your copy of PassPorter at http://www.passporter.com/register.asp, or you can send us a postcard or letter to P.O. Box 3880, Ann Arbor, Michigan 48106.

Report a Correction or Change

Keeping up with the changes at Walt Disney World is virtually impossible without your help. When you notice something is different than what is printed in PassPorter, or you just come across something you'd like to see us cover, please let us know! You can report your news, updates, changes, corrections, and even rumors (everything helps!) at http://www.passporter.com/wdw/report.asp.

Contribute to the Next Edition

You can become an important part of future editions of PassPorter! The easiest way is to rate the resorts, rides, and/or eateries at http://www.passporter.com/wdw/rate.htm. Your ratings and comments become part of our reader ratings throughout the book and help future readers make travel decisions. Want to get more involved? Send us a vacation tip or magical memory—if we use it in a future edition of PassPorter, we'll credit you by name in the guidebook and send you a free copy of the edition!

Get Your Questions Answered

We love to hear from you! Alas, due to the thousands of e-mails and hundreds of phone calls we receive each week we cannot offer personalized advice to all our readers. But there's a great way to get your questions answered: ask your fellow readers! Visit our message boards at http://www.passporterboards.com, join for free, and post your question. In most cases, fellow readers and Disney fans will offer their ideas and experiences! Our message boards also function as an ultimate list of frequently asked questions. Just browsing through to see the answers to other readers questions will reap untold benefit! This is also a great way to make friends and have fun while planning your vacation. But be careful—our message boards can be addictive!

PassPorter E-Books

Looking for more in-depth coverage on specific topics? Look no further than PassPorter E-Books! Our e-books are inexpensive (from $5.95–$8.95) and available immediately as a download on your computer (Adobe PDF format). If you prefer your books printed, we have options for that, too! And unlike most e-books, ours are fully formatted just like a regular PassPorter print book. A PassPorter e-book will even fit into a Deluxe PassPorter Binder, if you have one. We offer 12 e-books, at press time, and have plans for many, many more!

PassPorter's Disney 500: *Fast Tips for Walt Disney World Trips*
Our most popular e-book has more than 500 time-tested Walt Disney World tips—all categorized and coded! We chose the best of our reader-submitted tips over a six-year period for this e-book and each has been edited by author Jennifer Marx. For more details, a list of tips, and a sample page, visit http://www.passporter.com/wdw/disney500.asp.

PassPorter's Cruise Clues: *First-Class Tips for Disney Cruise Trips*
Get the best tips for the Disney Cruise Line—all categorized and coded—as well as cruise line comparisons, a teen perspective, and ultimate packing lists! This popular e-book is packed with 250 cruiser-tested tips—all edited by award-winning author Jennifer Marx. Visit http://www.passporter.com/dcl/cruiseclues.asp.

PassPorter's Disney Character Yearbook
A 268-page compendium of all the live Disney characters you can find at Walt Disney World, Disneyland, and on the Disney Cruise Line. Also includes tips on finding, meeting, photographing, and getting autographs, plus a customizable autograph book to print! Visit http://www.passporter.com/disney-character-yearbook.asp.

PassPorter's Disney Speed Planner: *The Easy Ten-Step Program*
A fast, easy method for planning practically perfect vacations—great for busy people or those who don't have lots of time to plan. Follow this simple, ten-step plan to help you get your vacation planned in short order so you can get on with your life. It's like a having an experienced friend show you the ropes—and have fun doing it! Visit http://www.passporter.com/wdw/speedplanner.asp.

PassPorter's Free-Book
A Guide to Free and Low-Cost Activities at Walt Disney World
It's hard to believe anything is free at Walt Disney World, but there are actually a number of things you can get or do for little to no cost. This e-book documents more than 150 free or cheap things to do before you go and after you arrive. Visit http://www.passporter.com/wdw/free-book.asp.

PassPorter's Sidekick for the Walt Disney World Guidebook

An interactive collection of worksheets, journal pages, and charts
This is a customizable companion to our general Walt Disney World guidebook—you can personalize worksheets, journals, luggage tags, and charts, plus click links to all the URLs in the guidebook and get transportation pages for all points within Walt Disney World! Details at http://www.passporter.com/wdw/sidekick.asp.

PassPorter's Festivals and Celebrations
at Walt Disney World

Get in on all the fun in this updated 78-page overview of all the wonderful and magical festivals, celebrations, parties, and holidays at Walt Disney World. Included are beautiful color photos and tips on maximizing your experience at the festivals and celebrations. Read more and see a sample page at http://www. passporter.com/wdw/festivals-celebrations.asp.

PassPorter's Answer Book

Get answers to the most popular topics asked about Walt Disney World, Disneyland, Disney Cruise Line, and general travel. You've asked it, we've answered it! The e-book's questions and answers are sorted geographically and topically. The e-book is authored by our amazing PassPorter Guide Team, who have heaps of experience at answering your questions! Details at http://www.passporter.com/answer-book.asp.

PassPorter's Disney Weddings & Honeymoons

This is both a guidebook and a bridal organizer tailored to the unique requirements of planning a wedding, vow renewal, or commitment ceremony at Walt Disney World or on the Disney Cruise Line. It will take you through the entire process, outline your options, offer valuable tips, organize your information, and help you plan your event down to the last detail! Get all the details at http://www.passporter.com/weddings.asp.

PassPorter's Disney Vacation Club Guide

A 170-page in-depth guide to all aspects of the Disney Vacation Club, from deciding whether to join to deciding where and when to use your points. Included are beautiful color photos and tips on maximizing your experience. If you've ever wondered what the club is all about or wanted to learn more, this is the perfect introduction. Details at http://www.passporter.com/disney-vacation-club.asp.

Learn more about these and other titles and order e-books at:
http://www.passporterstore.com/store/ebooks.aspx

PassPorter Online

A wonderful way to get the most from your PassPorter is to visit our active web site at http://www.passporter.com. We serve up valuable PassPorter updates, plus useful Walt Disney World information and advice we couldn't jam into our book. You can swap tales (that's t-a-l-e-s, Mickey!) with fellow Disney fans, play contests and games, find links to other sites, get plenty of details, and ask us questions. You can also order PassPorters and shop for PassPorter accessories and travel gear! The latest information on new PassPorters to other destinations is available on our web site as well.

PassPorter Web Sites	Address (URL)
Main Page: PassPorter Online	http://www.passporter.com
Walt Disney World Forum	http://www.passporter.com/wdw
PassPorter Posts Message Boards	http://www.passporterboards.com
Book Updates	http://www.passporter.com/customs/bookupdates.htm
Rate the Rides, Resorts, Restaurants	http://www.passporter.com/wdw/rate.htm
Register Your PassPorter	http://www.passporter.com/register.asp
PassPorter Deluxe Edition Information	http://www.passporter.com/wdw/deluxe.htm